The Dance Writings
of Carl Van Vechten

Carl Van Vechten, a self portrait

The Dance Writings of Carl Van Vechten

Edited, and with an Introduction by
PAUL PADGETTE

CENTENNIAL EDITION

DEDICATED TO THE MEMORY OF

CARL VAN VECHTEN

1880—1964

DANCE HORIZONS · NEW YORK

Copyright 1974 by Paul Padgette

All rights reserved. No part of this book may be reproduced
or utilized in any form or by any means, electronic or
mechanical, including photocopying, recording or by any
information storage and retrieval system, without permission
in writing from the Publisher.

ISBN 0-87127-114-1

Library of Congress Catalog Card Number 79-57139

Printed in the United States of America

First paperback edition 1980

Dance Horizons, 1801 East 26th Street
Brooklyn, NY 11229

The drawing on the cover is from
Carl Van Vechten's bookplate which was
designed by Prentiss Taylor.

Contents

vii : *Acknowledgements*   ix : *Introduction*

PART 1 — AMERICAN POTPOURRI

- 3 : Terpsichorean Souvenirs
- 10 : Interpretative Art
- 11 : Ballet in New York
- 12 : Metropolitan Opera Ballet
- 15 : Isadora Duncan
- 22 : The New Isadora, 1917
- 28 : An Appreciation
- 29 : Maud Allan, 1910
- 32 : Loie Fuller, 1909
- 34 : The Negro Theatre
- 38 : The Lindy Hop
- 40 : Nassau Dancing
- 42 : Eloquent Alvin Ailey
- 45 : Choreography for Americans
- 49 : Belief in an Ideal
- 52 : Terpsichore and The U.S. Army

PART 2 — RUSSIANS

- 59 : Secret of the Russian Ballet
- 79 : Waslav Nijinsky
- 95 : Anna Pavlowa and Mikail Mordkin, 1910
- 102 : Anna Pavlowa, 1920
- 104 : Swan Lake Ballet
- 107 : Igor Strawinsky
- 116 : Stage Decoration as a Fine Art

PART 3 — ALICIA MARKOVA

- 123 : Queen of the Dance
- 126 : Gardenias for Alicia

PART 4 — MUSIC AND DANCE ON THE IBERIAN PENINSULA

135 : The Land of Joy   *142* : Spain and Music

PART 5 — LÉO DELIBES

171 : Léo Delibes

179 : *Index*

PHOTOGRAPHS BY CARL VAN VECHTEN:

Frontispiece: Carl Van Vechten, a self portrait.
Nora Kaye as the Ballerina in *Petrouchka*.
Agnes de Mille in her own *Three Virgins and a Devil*, 1941. (Bruce Kellner Collection)
Bill Robinson, 1941. (Beinecke Library, Yale University)
Alvin Ailey.
John Kriza in Eugene Loring's *Billy the Kid*.
Alicia Markova and Milorad Miskovitch in *L'Après-midi d'un Faune*. (Bruce Kellner Collection)
Hugh Laing and Janet Reed in de Mille's *Tally-Ho*, 1944.
Martha Graham and Bertram Ross.
Paul Taylor in Balanchine's *Episodes*.
Anton Dolin in Fokine's *Bluebeard*.
Melissa Hayden. (Bruce Kellner Collection)
Violette Verdy.
Katherine Dunham, 1940.
Geoffrey Holder.
Jerome Robbins in de Mille's *Three Virgins and a Devil*, 1941.
Francisco Moncion.

All photographs not otherwise credited are in the collection of the Editor.

Nora Kaye as the Ballerina in Petrouchka

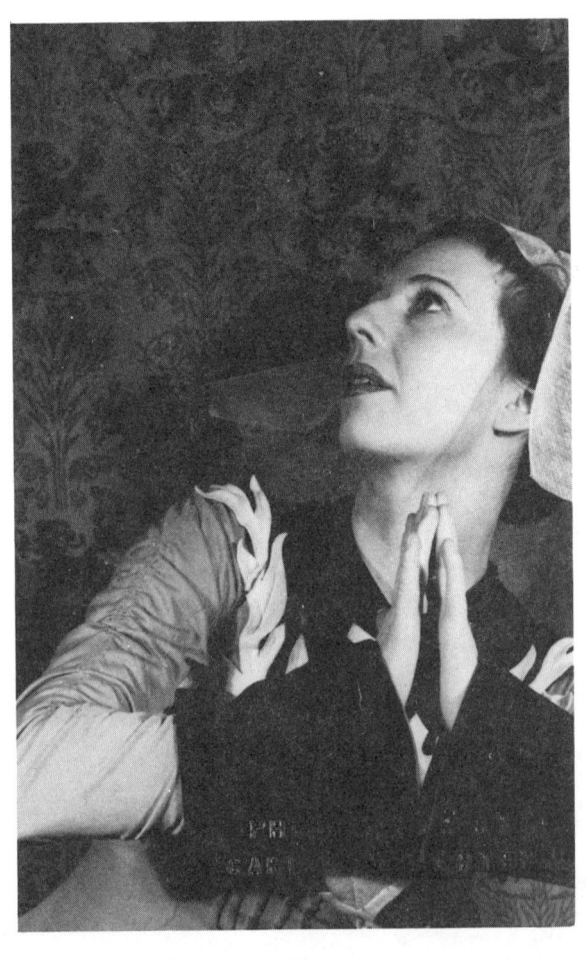

Agnes de Mille in her own
Three Virgins and a Devil, *1941*

Bill Robinson, 1941

Alvin Ailey

John Kriza in Eugene Loring's
Billy the Kid

*Alicia Markova and Milorad Miskovitch
in* L'Après-midi d'un Faune

Hugh Laing and Janet Reed in de Mille's Tally-Ho, *1944*

Martha Graham and Bertram Ross

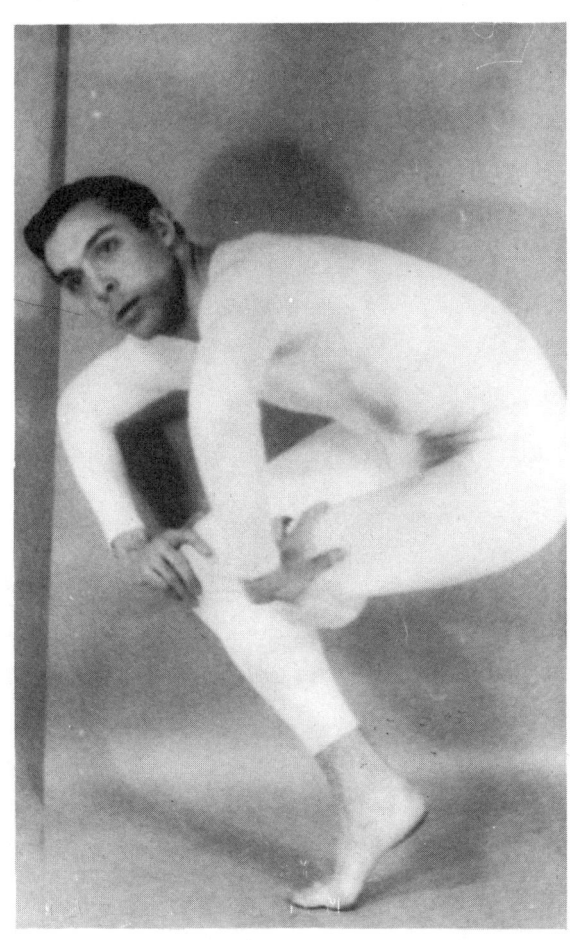

Paul Taylor in Balanchine's Episodes

Anton Dolin in Fokine's Bluebeard

Melissa Hayden

Violette Verdy

Katherine Dunham, 1940

Geoffrey Holder

Jerome Robbins in de Mille's
Three Virgins and a Devil, *1941*

Francisco Moncion

Acknowledgements

Two significant titles relating to Van Vechten's dance writing not mentioned elsewhere in this volume are: John Townsend Barrett's unpublished Columbia University thesis (1955), *Analysis and Significance of Three American Critics of the Ballet: Carl Van Vechten, Edwin Denby and Lincoln Kirstein*; an article by John Martin, "Carl Van Vechten, 1880-1964," which appeared in the January 9, 1965, number of the *New York City Ballet Program*, New York State Theatre.

There are two general bibliographies: Scott Cunningham (1924), and Klaus W. Jonas (1955) with "Additions," in *Papers of Bibliographical Society of America*, LV, First Quarter, 1961. Both are available in most libraries. Not so easy to find, but including information not available elsewhere, are Frank Paluka's *Iowa Authors: A Bio-Bibliography of Sixty Native Writers,* University of Iowa, 1967, with a chapter on Van Vechten, and my own catalogue, *Carl Van Vechten*, published at the time of a Memorial Exhibit at the San Francisco Public Library in 1965. For a number of years I have kept a progressive bibliography of Van Vechten's writing and photography, but there are no definite arrangements for its publication at the time of this writing.

Bruce Kellner has written what will undoubtedly remain the definitive biography until sealed material at The New York Public Library is released. It is *Carl Van Vechten & the Irreverent Decades,* University of Oklahoma Press, 1968. A fine article reviewing Van Vechten's career is "A Three-Quarter-Length Portrait of Carl Van Vechten," by James Ringo, published in the *Cabellian,* Vol.1, no. 2,1969.

I wish to acknowledge the cooperation of the late Fania Marinoff Van Vechten for her interest in the progress of this project. Thanks to Joseph Solomon, Van Vechten's executor, for permission to publish these works. Donald Gallup, Curator of American Literature, Yale University

Library and Van Vechten's literary trustee, has given me his encouragement and cooperation. For their permission to quote from them in the Introduction of this book, I am grateful to Clive Barnes, Arlene Croce, Edward Jablonski, Bruce Kellner, Lincoln Kirstein, Leo Lerman, Edward Lueders, Paul Magriel, and John Martin. I wish to thank John M. Vick for his translations of quotes from French appearing in the text.

The following publishers have granted permission to reprint excerpts from their copyrighted works: Alfred A. Knopf, *Dance Magazine,* Dance Perspectives Foundation, G. Schrimer, Inc., *The New York Times, The Saturday Review,* Vanguard Press, Inc., and W.C.C. Publishing Company (New York Herald Tribune, Inc.). *The New York Times* articles are © 1911/10/09 by The New York Times Company.

Special thanks is extended to Bruce Kellner, and the Beinecke Library at Yale University for their permission to use photographs in their possession for this book.

To Desmond Arthur, I wish to acknowledge my appreciation for his encouragement and assistance in preparing this manuscript.

San Francisco   Paul Padgette

Introduction

A large and important part of my life has been spent in the company of books. As a child, it was in reading them, either from my home shelves or from the library. Later, it took the form of collecting them. This passion led to the selling of books to other people sharing a similar addiction. At the university I had discovered an area in American literature that was not covered in the texts. I called it the American School of the Comedy of Manners. Beginning with Wycherley, England produced, among others, Sheridan, Peacock, Beerbohm, and more recently Firbank and Evelyn Waugh. Parallel names of this genre in American annals are scarce in quality and number. Some of the work of Edgar Saltus, James Huneker, and Stark Young qualifies; much of the fiction of Elinor Wylie is analogic, but the most notable of American Comedy of Manners writers is Carl Van Vechten.

In the Twenties, Carl Van Vechten wrote seven brittle, witty, and highly successful novels. Before that, beginning in 1915 and continuing for more than a decade, he published nine volumes of essays on music, drama, dance, and literature.

Ten years ago his books were to be found catching dust on bottom shelves in antiquarian bookshops, both in San Francisco, where I live, and in New York, as I found out on my first visit there in 1962. Frances Steloff's Gotham Book Mart was the only shop with a row of Van Vechten titles, properly displayed. Now, a decade later, they have nearly disappeared from the shelves, top or bottom ones. The multiple printings of his popular novels are nearly gone and the critical volumes are to be had, if at all, for high prices. Since his death in 1964 and the publication of Bruce Kellner's biography in 1968, the revival of interest in his work is increasing. This collection of his writing on dance is the first in bringing his important critical work back into print. Collections of his articles on music, drama, and literature could easily fill equal books. Virtually all of the material in this collection was published more than a quarter of a century ago and much of it twice that long ago. Indeed, some of it originally appeared in newspapers no longer in existence and in uncommon periodicals.

One of my first Van Vechten acquisitions was a battered copy of *Excavations* (1926), a critical collection mostly reprinted from earlier books and magazines. He often extended and re-worked magazine material for book publication. It was a fortunate discovery for me because it contained much of his best work. It included, for example, his essay on Léo Delibes, which is the concluding piece in the present collection. Most of Van Vechten's work as a reviewer and critic was over by 1920. In "A Valedictory," which prefaces a collection on music called *Red* (1925), he says: "When I was younger I held the firm belief that after forty (he was forty-five at the time) the cells hardened and that prejudices were formed which precluded the possibility of the welcoming of novelty. From almost the moment I began to write on the subject of music, therefore, I took it upon myself to attack the older men who had closed their minds to new ideas." And indeed he did! This collection on dance shows how he championed the new and revolutionary artists of the time, Stravinsky, Duncan, etc. — but he also respected the classic work of Spanish dance and Delibes. He was not afraid to voice unpopular opinions in his reviews and articles; he had integrity. Time has proven his views and opinions to be valid and they are acceptable today.

On that first visit to New York I spent many hours at the New York Public Library seeing the Carl Van Vechten Collection. It was fascinating both in mass and scope. I had arranged to visit Yale University Library the following week to pay homage to another literary figure: Gertrude Stein. This was a natural connection because Van Vechten, acting as Gertrude Stein's literary executor, had edited eight volumes of her unpublished writings for Yale. While examining with much pleasure many manuscripts, photographs, and letters, I also made the acquaintance of

Donald Gallup, Curator of American Literature at Yale, who is in charge of literary matters for both Gertrude Stein and Carl Van Vechten.

Reading the opening paragraphs of Gertrude Stein's *The Making of Americans* in manuscript was truly exciting for me — "Once an angry man dragged his father along the ground through his orchard. 'Stop!' cried the groaning old man at last, 'Stop! I did not drag my father beyond this tree.' "

My eagerness impressed Mr. Gallup to suggest that one so involved with Gertrude Stein's writing should meet Carl Van Vechten, who had been her friend, promoter, and self-proclaimed fan for thirty years. The idea had not occurred to me before that afternoon. The friendship with Van Vechten that followed our meeting a few days later was immediate and lasting. My gratitude to Donald Gallup is never-ending.

After I returned to San Francisco Van Vechten and I began a correspondence which averaged a letter a week between us until his death.

On my succeeding visits to New York, he would lay out an itinerary for me, "to complete my unadequate education," he was fond of saying. His continuing enthusiasm, his keen interest and immediate reaction to me and my activities was always flattering. More important here, it demonstrates his absorption with people and parallels his responsiveness to the wide spectrum of the performing arts, the new in writing, music and the fine arts. Throughout his critical writing this incredible, active interest is seen in his choice of words in describing a performance. In "The Land of Joy," in this collection, he writes of a dance performance thus: "Fortunately the Spaniards in the first-night audience gave the cue, unlocked the lips and loosened the hands of us cold Americans. For my part, I was soon yelling *Ole!* louder than anybody else."

Another facet of his personality both as a person and a writer is the catholic sweep of his subject matter. In an essay on the British writer M.P. Shiel, we learn some personal views of Hugh Walpole; in an article on actress Sophie Arnould are reflections on French culture; in reading about Oscar Hammerstein we are witness to firsthand impressions of New York and its theatres at the beginning of the century. At one point he exclaims almost as an apology: "I cannot resist further cataloguing." I suggest the reader will aid his enjoyment and understanding of Van Vechten by keeping an unabridged Oxford close by. In intimate fashion he shares his pleasures, discoveries, and revelations with you from the printed page. Critic Fanny Butcher in the Chicago *Tribune* has said ". . . the secret of the charm of his essays is that they're really very learned in material but not in the least bit in treatment."

In the middle of his essay on "Spain and Music," there is a diversion on Philip Thicknesse, a minor but fascinating English writer of the Eighteenth Century. It is difficult to read this passage without immediately rushing to your favorite bookshop to purchase several of the twenty-four books we are told Thicknesse wrote. Alas, the difficulty is that none are in print.

Paul Magriel, writing in 1947 said, "Carl Van Vechten is much like his Nineteenth Century predecessor, Théophile Gautier, at once storyteller, belle-lettrist and the major dance critic of his time."[1]

The career of Carl Van Vechten was so many-sided that to discuss and separate one part from another poses a problem in chronology. His writing on dance was some of his earliest work for the New York *Times*. Reading it we can follow his development as a writer. In the first article in this collection, written in 1956, he says there was no set of rules for dance criticism in the first decade of the century. Most of the formal expressions used to describe movement in dance were yet uncoined by Van Vechten or anyone else. Clive Barnes paid tribute to him in 1969: ". . . the first battles for responsible dance criticism were fought by a few pioneers such as Cyril Beaumont and Arnold Haskell in England, Carl Van Vechten and John Martin in America . . . ."[2] The custom of the day left reviews unsigned. Indeed, the first-line music critics cared not to vary from the comfortable routine of opera, concert, and symphony reviewing to cover the dance. As an associate music critic on the *Times*, Van Vechten was assigned the dance programs by default. What he did was characteristic. He took the throw-away assignment and made it into a feature piece. Bruce Kellner says it well. "Richard Aldrich demurred, in favor of his assistant, and Carl Van Vechten was put in the fortuitous position of becoming America's first dance critic."[3] His reputation grew as a writer on dance and by the time he officially retired from the field in 1920, he was generally considered the leading critic on dance in New York. Edwin Denby, himself a contender for this title, called him "our greatest ballet critic."[4]

He had history on his side. Only three years after joining the *Times* and six years out of the University of Chicago, he was to witness within a few months the American debuts of Pavlova and Mordkin from Russia, Maud Allan's first New York showing, the first important New York performance by Isadora Duncan, and Loie Fuller's return to New York after European successes. He not only saw them, he wrote about them. These newspaper reviews lack the polish and style to be found in the later, longer, detailed articles on Nijinsky and the Russian Ballet. The short, chronological reportage of the Duncan performances (1909-1911) and the 1917 essay, "The New Isadora," if read side by side, reveal interesting and startling changes in both the writing of Van Vechten and the dancing of Isadora. The same development toward maturity in writing would be evident in comparing his early writings on opera and drama with the kind of piece in which he later excelled, the "personal essay," a species barely visible today.

Compare these lines on Isadora: "She is at her best in dances which depict life and gaiety and motion. In this she is always sure of communicating her meaning to an audience." (1909). By 1911 he was not certain of Isadora's purpose; he concluded a review concerning the dancer's interpretation of *Liebestod*: "Miss Duncan's conception of the music did not seem to suggest a pantomimic Isolde, nor was it exactly dancing. In other words, she puzzled those who knew the music drama, and did not interest those who did not. Therefore one may ask, Why?" In his longer essay in 1917 Van Vechten was saying: "The incipient dancer keeping her feet pure for her coming marriage with her art is a subject for philosophic dissertation or for poetry...she remained faithful to her original ideal, the beauty of abstract movement, the rhythm of exquisite gesture...part of her effect is gained by gesture, part by the massing of her body, but the greater part by facial expression." In this last article he admits that in the earlier exposures to Isadora's art "... (it) said nothing to me, but eventually I began to take pleasure in watching it." It would seem that both Isadora and Van Vechten improved with exposure and practice in their personal arts.

In writing a "comment" to a selection of Van Vechten's dance criticism published by *Dance Index* in 1942, John Martin observed: "The newspaper reviews, however, are characterized by the quick and accurate first judgements of an artist who happened also to be an excellent newspaper man, and...constitute as brilliant a critical document as one is likely to find... The reviews he then wrote...form a body of criticism that is an uncommonly valuable contribution to America's literature in that field."[5]

During the period he was writing about dance, whether ballet, Spanish folk-dances, Broadway musicals or Negro inventions such as the Lindy Hop, he was also writing on other forms of music. In 1917, he wrote his magnificent articles on Nijinsky and Isadora Duncan. During the same year, he published provocative essays on Mary Garden, Philip Moeller, and a pioneer article on the use of music with silent movies called "Music and the Electrical Theater." Edward Lueders, Van Vechten's first biographer, has said in the *New Republic* that he was "a singular figure in Twentieth Century America with multiple contributions to its culture and its animation."[6]

According to Scott Cunningham in *Bibliography of Carl Van Vechten* in 1924, the contributions to the New York *Times* beween 1906 and 1913 were enough to fill ten "very large scrap books." In 1913-1914 Van Vechten was drama critic for the New York *Press,* writing both daily and Sunday. He was, one summer, editorial writer for the New York *Globe,* writing two or three editorials a day for a period of three months. During the same period, he occasionally contributed pieces on dance and music to the *Globe.* Included in this collection is his "Ballet in New York," a *Globe* piece from 1911. Beginning in 1916, he contributed both signed and unsigned pieces for most of Alfred A Knopf's catalogues. Knopf had just begun publishing and was to bring out all Van Vechten's books except his first, *Music After the Great War,* published in 1915 by G. Schirmer. In 1920, playwright Philip Moeller, said: "His chief concern has been with interpretations and interpreters. Taking the one or the other as his theme, he has written critical variations and the result has been critical creation." [7]

Keeping pace with his writing development were his collecting instincts. In order to collect material for a new feature, he not only did research in the New York Public Library, but he acquired sizable collections of books on the subject. In later years, these same books were to form the nucleus of institutional collections, which he would help establish and fund. These are as varied as everything else about him. They include photograph collections (his own photographs) of dancers, singers, actors, and writers as well as literary collections on Negro history and literature, cats, music and musical literature, and books on the fine arts. One of the most revealing symbolic representations of Van Vechten is Florine Stettheimer's 1922 portrait of him. In it he is centrally seated, charming, sophisticated, worldly, surrounded by his preoccupations: theatrical draperies, a piano, typewriter, a cat perched on several of his own books, a theatre marquee with the name of Fania Marinoff, his actress wife, a figure representing him as a cook, with the *cordon-bleu*.

"His criticisms of the dance. . .are an important source of information on the period and helped to popularize dance in the United States." So said Anatole Chujoy in *Dance Encyclopedia*.

In reading these pieces on dance, so far removed from the world in which they were written, it is useful to place in perspective some of the characteristics of the period. It was a time of immense change in all the arts. In painting, cubism was making its first appearances in France at the same time as Van Vechten was first writing about Isadora, Pavlova and *Swan Lake*. He published his first book only two years after the revolutionary Armory Show in 1913 in New York which changed art appreciation in the United States. Alfred Stieglitz had opened the Little Galleries of the Photo-Secession at 291 Fifth Avenue, where the new bohemians mingled. Further down the street, Mabel Dodge, at Number 23, held court for many of the same people, including Van Vechten, at her celebrated salons. *Salome* was being sung by Mary Garden at the Manhattan Opera House in 1909 at almost the same time as Pavlova danced several blocks away. Each lady in her way caused a sensation.

In our view, the novels of the day were less sophisticated than the performing arts. The best seller in 1909, according to Alice Payne Hacket's *50 Years of Best Sellers*, was *The Inner Shrine* by Basil King. In 1911 the New York Public Library was opened at Fifth Avenue and 42nd Street. It was the beginning of the era of the "little magazine." *Poetry* magazine began publication in 1912 in Chicago; *The Little Review* began in 1914. Van Vechten edited his own *Trend* from 1912 to 1914 and a short lived one called *Rongwrong* in 1917. Copies of both magazines are rare today.

Van Vechten's essays are a summary review of the intellectual thinking of the times; they are also a rendering of its gossip. The more one knows about the subject the more one enjoys the writing; the less one knows about the subject the more one will want to learn. Our understanding is enlarged when we can grasp the extent to which he sought for exact ideas, the correct word. He depends on the reader to attend, consider, and eventually, to agree — after considerable "cataloguing" in support of his view. He knew he was a pioneer in much of his critical writing. He expects us to learn along with him. Lincoln Kirstein, in his eulogy on Van Vechten, remembered: "From Carl I learned the elegance in the ordinary. I first saw an American ballet had to have more to do with sport and jazz than czars and ballerinas." [8]

Many admirers of Van Vechten have voiced the theory that although he officially stopped writing on the dance, it did not affect his attendance or his influence and candid opinions on the subject. In an article that touched on this theme, Edward Jablonski in 1960 said: "His enthusiasm for the works of others is rare and extraordinarily selfless."[9]

In his two reviews on the autobiography of Agnes de Mille, included in this book, he quotes her at length on the subject of Martha Graham; in so doing both pay respect and express admiration for the great dancer. It is typical of Van Vechten's way of expressing his feelings for a creative artist.

In a letter to me on October 27, 1963, he wrote a capsule essay: "Yesterday I attended Martha Graham's dances for the second time. I am more than ever impressed by this lady. I believe her to be the greatest living choreographer. The others all work over old material, but she invents all her material and every time she creates a new dance she creates new material. Not only that she invents new twists to the old stories she uses and the new twists are brilliant...Her dancers follow her every behest with remarkable energy and zest. I am mad for the whole business and I think her latest ballet, *Judith*, is her greatest to date." Six months later, on April 8, 1964, he wrote: "I saw a perfectly extraordinary performance by Martha Graham's troup in which they demonstrated the details of how they learned their technique." Three months earlier, January 29, 1964, he wrote me the following impressions of a young dancer that express the same kind of magnificent ardor he felt fifty years earlier for Pavlova and Nijinsky. "I have become deeply interested in a young dancer of the New York City Ballet named Mimi Paul. I believe she has more talent than anyone else I have seen since Markova. I am wildly enthusiastic about her. She is especially incredible in a Japanese ballet of Balanchine called *Bugaku*. Watching her in this I fall into a dream trance."

Arlene Croce, editor of *Ballet Review*, evaluating influences on her career wrote: "...when a critic's standards are of the highest, as Van Vechten's were, his subject never dies — it just keeps translating itself as the years pass. And of course Van Vechten's descriptions of Nijinsky's own performances are matchless." [10]

His ardent admiration for the young creative person was crucial in keeping his critical opinion vital. In January, 1963, lamenting the death of an old friend, he wrote to me that "most of my old friends have passed or are passing, but I have so many young friends, they keep me feeling young and alive." He said that the quality of novelty is most often found in the young performer. Therefore, interpretation is dependent on the performer's ability to invent that kind of stage business which will excite and please an audience. Even at the expense of mechanical skill, which may leave him unmoved, the performer must project a special quality to define him from all others. Van Vechten refers to this as a quality of being *intimate*. He applied this to both the performer and the writer. I once told him that intimacy in writing required great courage as it revealed so much of the person; he responded in typical form. "Being intimate does not take courage, but it does take experience...I have never been anything else, writing letters or writing books. In fact all good writers are intimate."

In 1961, Leo Lerman published a long article in the New York *Times* called "Dance: June Walk" in which the subject of intimacy and creation is discussed. "He wrote about dance straight from a huge heart filled with love of the art, and he wrote from an exquisite but lusty sensibility fortified by an encyclopedic knowledge of the most esoteric subjects...(his) basic concern...in writing about dance...has always been to capture and communicate essences, individualities, what makes a great artist, a great performer. In reading Van Vechten you can see how Nijinsky danced, what Isadora Duncan really was like...Recently I asked him about Performance as an element in great art. What is so important about Performance? 'It is,' Mr. Van Vechten said, 'dancing from inside. Actually no dancer can learn to dance from inside. That is why Nijinsky was so much greater than any male dancer of the period. There are people who have love inside and can't project. It has to come from the inside. It cannot be learned.' "[11]

He had a continuing interest throughout his life in all phases of the arts; the emphasis changed from time to time, but the initial involvement never waned. He was not averse to expressing strong opinions on matters large and small. In the Fall of 1962 he wrote me that "the new Philharmonic Hall, of which you have probably heard even in San Francisco, is a disappointment. The acoustics are awful and the band sounds as if it were playing under water, or under a wet blanket. Also there is practically no place to pee and you have to walk about a mile before you can accomplish this act. The spaces are fabulous and the staircases numberless. The place is all Glamour and makes no SENSE."

As far as I know, the last thing he wrote relating to dance was in the form of a printed invitation to an exhibit of painted portraits by Richard Banks of twenty members of the New York City Ballet. The exhibit opened with the ballet season in March, 1963, and the invitation read as follows. "Richard Banks, once a composer of note, then a painter of rank, latterly a painter of portraits, has some of his more recent work — a document of the New York City

Ballet Company — here for your inspection, and for your obvious approval." In a letter to me on March 15, he described that the season opened "very brilliantly indeed."

In spite of his years of writing he suffered as do many writers from inertia. In a letter listing things he had been doing that would stagger one half his age, he continued with this confession: "I work consistently on photography and I have some writing I must do, but I keep putting it off. I always prefer to write letters or to get drunk or whatever. I HATE to write. Curiously enough some of my best writing has actually been accomplished when I have been ill." At another time he wrote: "My life is tangled with a ridiculous amount of work. The publisher of the Florine Stettheimer book is howling, baying, screaming for my preface." At the beginning of the New York newspaper strike in December, 1962, he commented, "We have had no newspapers for a week and as I never listen to the radio I am totally ignorant of world affairs and don't even know what theatres are open. It is a blissful feeling."

One Christmas season he wrote: "I am busy as a bird dog, writing, taking photographs and printing them, attending all the cocktail and other rites of the Christmas season and carrying on generally . . . The week continues to be filled up with food and drink in excelsis. I always take three months off free from food or liquor after Christmas. I am a MONK. . .Thanks for your letters and telegram, and with very warm greetings, I leave you and return to the treadmill."

August 1973   Paul Padgette

1. Magriel: preface to *Pavlova,* Holt, 1947.
2. Barnes: "PW Manchester: An Appreciation With Love," *Dance News*, October, 1969.
3. Kellner: *Carl Van Vechten & the Irreverent Decades*, University of Oklahoma Press, 1968.
4. Denby: *Looking At The Dance*, Pellegrini & Cudahy, 1949.
5. Martin: *Dance Index* (Sept-Oct-Nov), 1942.
6. Lueders: "Mr Van Vechten of New York City," *New Republic*, May 16, 1955.
7. Moeller: "Van Vechten," *The Borzoi 1920*, Knopf, 1920.
8. Kirstein: Eulogy spoken at memorial service, December, 1964.
9. Jablonski: "Carlo Patriarch," *American Record Guide*, June, 1960.
10. Croce: "Dance Books in My Life," *Dance Magazine*, March, 1969.
11. Lerman: "Dance:June Walk," *The New York Times*, June 18, 1961.

Editor's note: After considerable thought I have decided to retain the spelling of names of persons and titles of works exactly as they appear in the original publications as written by Van Vechten. When there is any obvious confusion the more recent rendering of the names is explained in a footnote.

1

American Potpourri

*"A dancer who is at once
literate and articulate may be
considered a novelty."*

Terpsichorean Souvenirs

I may have seen dancing earlier, but my first memory of the art takes me back to about 1892 when I would have been twelve years old and the dance of the period I saw and remember was the Skirt Dance, as it was fantastically called in those far-off days. The Skirt Dance was derived, of course, from the more obscene Can-Can, the form in which it still survives. My first view of the Skirt Dance was in Cedar Rapids, Iowa, in the crypt of Grace Episcopal Church, during an amateur performance of a popular operetta of the period, *1492*. In the original production of this musical there had been a ballet, but, on this occasion, this ballet had been metamorphosed into a solo by Herbie Newell, a Cedar Rapids youth, about sixteen at the time, I would imagine, who excelled in female impersonation. For the most part, the Skirt Dance, like its elder sister, the Can-Can, consisted of a progression of kicks and the preparation for these. However, the skirt was longer than that for the Can-Can, and fuller. In fact, Herbie manipulated thirty or forty yards of soft material, ankle length. What has become of him? I haven't heard of him for fifty or sixty years, but in 1892 he was headed for the Broadway stage and stardom.

I believe it was Lottie Collins, a popular London Music Hall star, who introduced the Skirt Dance as an accompaniment to a song which she made as familiar as "Yes, We Have No Bananas" became at a later day. I never saw Lottie Collins, but the song and her dance often turned up at Greene's Opera House in Cedar Rapids in the Hoyt farces and the Hanlon Brothers' extravaganzas, *Fantasma* and *Superba*, yearly visitors to the one-night stands in the Middle West.

My next vivid memory of the dance is of performances by Little Egypt on the Midway of the Columbian Exposition of the Chicago World's Fair in 1893. She was seen, naturally, in the Arabian *Dance du Ventre* and my principle recollection is of her dexterity with an apple, which hung by a cord from her belt and the spectacular motion of which she promoted by the muscular movements she produced around her belly. Unlike the Skirt Dance, which had even a more wicked ancestry, the *Dance du Ventre* was regarded as a very sinful exhibition, an idea emphasized by the immense amount of fleshy exposure.

In 1896, when I spent a winter in Cincinnati, I was introduced to the performances of La Loie Fuller, an American woman who had become the rage of Paris and who had even won over Camille Flammarion, the popular astronomer. In this first American tour she showed us the gems of her limited repertory: the Fire Dance, The Lily, and the others. She borrowed the skirt of the Skirt Dance, exaggerated it to insane proportions, one hundred yards of enveloping silk, exercised by iron rods into terrific aerial excesses. La Loie was sufficiently occupied with the propulation of these rods so that she scarcely moved her feet at all and then it was only sufficiently to slightly alter her position on the stage. The required effects, however, were generally achieved by the lighting which came from all directions, but particularly from below. By this extraordinarily skillful employment of electricity, novel in this gaslight era, La Loie was able to convince us that her draperies were aflame or that she was the center of an enormous calla lily that protruded into the flies. Later stage lighting was probably encouraged by La Loie, who might be called the great grandmother of the very great contemporary Jean Rosenthal.

Some years later La Loie appeared at the Metropolitan Opera House with a large company of soloists. Her drapery dances were now old hat, having been extensively imitated by aerial butterflies on wires (you may still see these nymphs of the air in circuses). On this occasion her young ladies seemed to be dancing under the influence of the recent inventions of Isadora Duncan. La Loie introduced herself in a "new dance of the hands," which she performed in a box (only her hands were visible) about the size of a Punch and Judy show. This exhibition might have been more effective in a smaller theatre.

Probably the next dancer to make a deep impression on me was the really great George Walker (of the team of Williams and Walker), who performed the cakewalk, actually a folk-dance, with his wife, Aida Overton Walker. This assuredly is one of the great memories of the theatre. The line, the grace, the assured ecstacy of these dancers, who bent over backward until their heads almost touched the floor, a feat demanding an incredible amount of strength, their enthusiastic prancing, almost in slow motion, have never been equalled in this particular revel, let alone surpassed. The cakewalk has been revived by several modern performers and choreographers, but never successfully except in *Shuffle Along* (the song was "I'm Just Wild About Harry"), and even there it was only a faint copy of the great Walker's thrilling performance. Most of the subsequent and current representations of the cakewalk were and are as authentic as Mae West would be in *Les Sylphides*.

In 1907, I went abroad for the first time and my first experience with dancing in London was at the Alhambra in Leicester Square, where a mediocre dancer named Alexia appeared in a mediocre ballet entitled *The Queen Of Spades*. It was my first visit to an English music hall and I was more fascinated by the brilliantly caparisoned ladies of pleasure who strolled back and forth in the promenade than I was by the action on the stage. Later, Alexia danced in New York at Hammerstein's Victoria. Adeline Genée at the Empire, likewise in Leicester Square, followed Alexia straight on in *Sir Rogerly de Coverly*, and I was captivated by the verve, the vitality, the liveliness and wit of Genée's toes; but even at this period I demanded more in the way of technique. Later, she, too, appeared in America, but in the end I tired of the verve as not too convincing. An enchanting personality remained.

The same year, in Munich, Olive Fremstad introduced me to the art of Isadora Duncan, which certainly held me enthralled and to which I remained faithful until she died.

It is my opinion that unless you have seen Isadora herself, you have never seen Duncan dancing. Her pupils, her "children," gave but pale reflections of her thrilling performances. The movements were frequently identical, but they did not capture one iota of the great woman's spirit. I can, however, add little to what I have already written about this great dancer and personality, who even influenced the Russians — who *especially* influenced the Russians.

Regina Badet may have been the next important dancer to come my way. Badet danced at the Opéra-Comique in Paris, where she was especially delightful in Massenet's *Manon*, in which, in the Cours-la-Reine scene, she was as delicate and graceful as a bit of Dresden china or Sevres which had come to life. In *Aphrodite*, which introduced me to Mary Garden, Badet took plastic poses on a table, quite nude inside a circle of gold, which contrived to assist her to look clothed or to appear even more naked, according to the spectator's point of view.

At about the same time I observed Madame Zambelli at the Opéra in, I believe, *Thaïs,* with the beautiful Lina Cavalieri singing the title role. Madame Zambelli was a fine dancer on the *pointes* and was much admired by amateurs of the genre, but her slenderness, which was extreme (how many slender dancers I have admired since that time!), together with her unusual height, served to disillusion me (a novice, then, before this kind of dancing). Further, she wore a tutu in this North African ballet set in a remote period, as was formerly the custom at the Opéra, even in *Tannhäuser,* another convention with which I was then unfamiliar.

In fact, I was almost totally ignorant of the finer points of any kind of dancing when suddenly, by default, I was thrown into the position of dance critic on the New York *Times*. Mr. Richard Aldrich, my senior in the music department, began by assigning me to dance performances, probably because he did not care to go himself.

What began in this manner as an accident was confirmed by custom. I was thus thrown into an important position (how important I did not realize for some time) at a period at which the dance unexpectedly emerged to become an important force in American life. I knew as much or more about dancing than most of my journalist friends, many of whom were ignorant even of prominent dancers' names, and whose standard of comparison was Albertina Rasch of the Hippodrome company. They could be of no assistance to me. Looking around for a crutch, I visited the New York Public Library, where I had often sought aid from the music department (which aided me immeasurably in the preparation of later books). However, succor, so far as the ballet was concerned, had to be meagre, as the shelves were weak in works pertaining to the dance. I found a very few, mostly in foreign tongues, about dancers long since gone to their graves. Up-to-date material on the subject was difficult to come by except from abroad. Some of the older books I was not yet prepared to understand.

There was nothing for an ambitious young critic to do but to educate himself in the subject and to invent his own descriptive terms, and that is what I proceeded to do.

Fortunately, for me, it was an excellent time to educate myself. Dancers sprang up in every direction. My early attempts at criticism were contemporary with the rage for Salome dancers (both play and opera were popular). Perhaps Maud Allen was the Queen of Salome dancers. I saw her, but I have no remembrance of her at all. On the other hand, Ruth St.Denis' Hindu dances I admired intensely and recall with enthusiasm.

From this time on dancers piled so thick and fast over my consciousness that I am confused about their order. Certainly Pavlova, when she appeared at the Metropolitan Opera House, captured my admiration and my lasting attention. I know now what I did not understand then, that she was deficient in some important technical particulars and that she did not always meticulously follow a choreographer's design (who does?), but at the time she seemed so perfect and was so brilliant in so many different ways that I speedily presented her with a wild youthful enthusiasm and very willingly forgot her lack of discipline. I made it my business to attend her every performance and to become acquainted with her during her first season here. I saw a good deal of her in her suite at the Knickerbocker Hotel and elsewhere. Naturally, I met Mordkin (whom I also admired, not having yet seen Nijinsky). The principal characteristic of his dancing, I learned with some rapidity, was a kind of athletic masculinity.

I have read somewhere that Spessivtzeva, the great Spessivtzeva, who has become a myth in the dancing world since she went mad, was in an early Russian company to dance in America. I have no memory of the lady or of the event. I did see Katerina Geltzer in a "complete" *Swan Lake*, but I was ignorant of both score and choreography at that time (try to imagine that state of affairs), and have no idea what was left out. Probably the thirty-two *fouettés* to begin with.

All this time I must have been learning little by little, about dancing, because when I was eventually exposed to Diaghilev's Ballet Russe in Paris, I was literally knocked over — I was certain I had never seen anything like it before. It was the second season I observed. Pavlova was no longer a member of this group, but Nijinsky was, and Karsavina. I recognized Karsavina at once for what she always remained for me, a dancer of great charm, but NOT a great ballerina. Nijinsky, on the other hand, completely effaced the memory of all the male dancers I had previously seen and indeed made such an indelible impression on me that I have never forgotten him and ever since have been comparing him with other male dancers to their detraction.

What I saw thereafter of the Russian Ballet was considerable, but a little difficult to place in space and time. Certainly I saw Massine in the *Legend of Joseph*, the Stravinsky ballets, including *Sacre du Printemps, Daphnis and Chloe* (however, with Fokine in place of Nijinsky); much later with Lifar, at the Paris Opéra; and very recently with the Sadler's Wells Company in New York; but by that time the glamour and magic of the first performances had disappeared along with Bakst's very beautiful costumes.

Now between 1910 (the date Markova was born) and 1920 (shortly before she made her début with Diaghilev), I wrote extensively about the ballet, still with some difficulty. I was now more familiar with some French texts and the Paris newspaper reviewers of the Russian Ballet, but I still was ignorant of the proper technical terms with which to describe certain dance steps and was obliged to invent my own. When Nijinsky was seen here in a *divertissement* called the *Princesse Enchantée*. I had no means of knowing that this was the celebrated set of variations called *The Blue Bird*, from the final act of *The Sleeping Beauty*. I had never heard of *volés brisés*. So I took my description of the impression Nijinsky made on me from the Book of Proverbs: "He winketh with his eyes, he speaketh with his feet, he teacheth with his fingers." Perhaps readers of my articles on the dance will recall other examples of similar verbal ingenuity.

Most of my writing on the ballet was accomplished by 1930, when the new dance collection was opened in the New York Public Library, which has proven so valuable a source of information for dancers, writers on the dance and balletomanes. Alas, it could no longer be of use to me.

The material in this article was included in Carl Van Vechten's Keynote Speech given at the Fifth Annual Capezio Award Luncheon. It was held at the St. Regis Roof on March 7, 1956. The award was presented by Van Vechten to Miss Genevieve Oswald, curator of Dance Archives at The New York Public Library. The speech was printed in *Dance Magazine*, January, 1957.

Interpretative Art

Interpretative Art...depends upon the contemporary individual, and some of its most thrilling effects may be entirely accidental. Any traditions which persist in interpretative art must be carried in the memory. In exceptional cases, of course, a singer, a dancer, or an actor is able to so stamp his or her personal achievement into the flowing rhythm of artistic space that a *style* does persist. We have a very good example before us in the case of Isadora Duncan, who has been followed by a long train of animated Grecian urns. The deleterious effect of this persistence of an interpretative tradition must be apparent to any one. For the imitator of an interpreter is a thousand times more futile than the imitator of a creator. Fortunately, on the whole, styles in acting, in singing, and in dancing frequently change.

— From "Epilogue," in *Interpreters*, Knopf, 1920.

Ballet In New York

The production of a number of Russian ballets hereabouts has aroused some degree of critical interest, which has expressed itself with more misconceptions than would be regarded as possible of so definite and limited a subject. We are told that the ballet – in its conventional form – has never been popular in New York. And yet in 1842 Fanny Elssler took $148,000 away from America. She danced innumerable times in New York to enormous and enthusiastic audiences. Without citing other instances at wearisome length, it is enough to mention the recent success of Pavlova and Mordkin, who actually drew larger audiences year before last to the Metropolitan Opera House than any operas or any singers of the year. Their success continues undiminished. The fact is, the ballet is just as popular here as it is elsewhere when great dancers trip into our ken.

We are further informed that Rimsky-Korsakow's *Scheherazade* is a ballet suite. The composition is so well known to concert-goers as a symphonic suite — Gustav Mahler was the last man to conduct it here in concert — that it would seem as if even the humblest writer for the papers might have discovered as much. In its original form it is programme music, and depicts some of the "Arabian Nights" tales as told by Scheherazade. With almost diabolical cleverness a Russian ballet master has fashioned the present ballet from it, which relates the events of the "Arabian Nights" previous to the appearance of Scheherazade. The original music is used without a change, except for the fact that the third section is omitted. Rimsky-Korsakow is dead, but his widow has publicly protested on several occasions against the use of her husband's music for this purpose.

But perhaps the supreme error has been made by an evening contemporary, which speaks of *Les Sylphides* as a revival of the ballet in which Taglioni was most famous. Misinformation, it would seem, has reached the acme in this statement. Taglioni won her greatest triumph in a ballet called *La Sylphide,* a work in two acts, with a definite story, the scenes of which are laid in Scotland. The music, which was of no value, was written by a forgotten composer named Schneitzhoeffer. The book was by the tenor Adolphe Nourrit.

Les Sylphides of present fame was arranged by one of the Russian ballet masters within the last three years. It is a collection of Chopin dances, orchestrated and strung together with no dramatic connection. With *La Sylphide* it has nothing more to do than with the Eiffel Tower or the Spanish Armada.

— *The New York Evening Globe,* June 28, 1911

Metropolitan Opera Ballet

The Metropolitan Opera House is to have a ballet composed entirely of American girls inside of two years. Mme. Cavallazzi, the head of the ballet school of that institution, said so yesterday at the exercises terminating the first year of the school. Twenty-four girls, most of them just sixteen years old, showed that it is not only Italians and French and Russians who can stand on their toes and pirouette.

"Mr. Gatti-Casazza came to me just before he sailed," said Mme. Cavallazzi, "and engaged ten of my girls after seeing them dance. He is only bringing eighteen girls from Europe this year, and next season the ballet will almost surely be made up entirely of American girls. Mr. Dippel came to me yesterday for girls for his Chicago opera company. I had none ready then which were not promised, but I'll have more in the Fall.

"I am greatly pleased with the success of my school, and I am sure that it will be even more of a success when I have had the girls longer. It is impossible to take girls here before they are sixteen on account of the law, and it is difficult to train première danseuses at that age, but it is possible to make the girls into coryphées if they are studious, and mine have been of that class."

The twenty-four girls in the class went through a regular programme yesterday in the rehearsal room of the Metropolitan Opera House, which was filled with spectators for the occasion.

Each of the girls was dressed in the conventional white ballet skirt, and most of them wore fillets of pink in their hair and pink tights. They were all of them pretty, and as the dancing took place in the daylight none of them was made up.

At the command of their instructor the girls lined up on the stage, and first went through a drill showing the first elementary exercises. Then they went on through various stages of dancing, and the audience greeted every pause with enthusiastic applause. Balancing on one leg they twirled the other through the air with remarkable lightness, and they bounded about the stage as if they had been doing it all their lives.

The conclusion of the afternoon's entertainment was a small divertissement, in which Miss Eva Swain, one of the youngest of the pupils, did a solo, after which she was greeted with such insistent applause that she came very near having to do it all over again. In the course of this dance Miss Swain jumped backward on one foot, with her other foot pointed at right angles behind her, one of the feats with which Pavlowa aroused great admiration last Winter.

After it was all over Mme. Cavallazzi received the congratulations of those present, and ice cream and cake were served by the ballet girls.

Mme. Cavallazzi was a famous dancer in her day. She appeared one year at the Metropolitan Opera House about twenty-five years ago, and her elopement with Charles Mapleson, a son of the famous impresario, was the cause of much excitement at the time. The dancer never returned to this country after the elopement until she came to open this ballet school last Fall. She intends to stay near New York in the Summer, and will reopen her school in the Fall.

— *The New York Times,* June 29, 1910

Isadora Duncan

Editor's Note: The modern reader of these reviews of Isadora Duncan's performances may be impressed by the excessive length of her programs and those of Maud Allan, Loie Fuller, Pavlova, and others. The choice of music seems no less surprising. Concert and theatre programs at the same period were similarly padded and lengthy. However, many and extensive cuts were made in pieces which if performed whole would have been impossible. Van Vechten's review of Pavlova's program of October 16, 1910, (later in this volume) mentions such cuts. In Duncan's case, in particular, the character of her music, her "borrowings" from the classics, is today no longer in fashion. Her *approach* to dance, however, has influenced most dancers ever since her time. Much of the standard repertoire of today was not written at the time these dancers performed. The early reviews and essays are valuable, historically, because they give us *word* pictures of important dancers in an era when dance criticism was scant, to say the least. They perform, in part, the function we may now call upon from film for records of performances. These words by Van Vechten, in many cases, are our only knowledge of the event. The fact they were written by a man who, often brilliantly, *shows* us the dancer and his interpretation — and frequently in newspaper reviews written in haste to meet deadlines — is more than reason enough to preserve them for the future.

Miss Isadora Duncan, who has evolved a style of choreographic art which corresponds in a measure at least — according to a comparison with the figures on ancient vases — with the dances of the ancient Greeks, made her reappearance in New York last evening at the Metropolitan Opera House, assisted by Walter Damrosch and the

New York Symphony Orchestra.[1]

The programme stated that Miss Duncan would dance to the ballets and choruses of Gluck's *Iphigénie en Aulide*. Most of her dances were accomplished to such aid, but at least one of them, a Chorus of Priestesses, was taken from *Iphigénie en Tauride*, and its original purpose and signification were greatly distorted by the dancer. It is a number which was never designed for dancing, and to any one who has heard it in its proper place in the opera it must seem more or less of a sacrilege to have it put to such purpose.

There can be no possible objection, however, to Miss Duncan's appropriating the ballet numbers from the Gluck operas for her particular purpose. It is a well known fact that Gluck composed many of his ballets because they were demanded by the audiences of his time rather than by the exigencies of his operas. It is also quite as true that the list of them includes much that is best of the Gluck music.

They are particularly fitted in their nobility and lack of sensuousness to accompany the moods and poses which Miss Duncan portrays in her dances. She is at her best in dances which depict life and gaiety and motion. In this she is always sure of communicating her meaning to an audience. The Bacchanale which ended the formal programme exhibited her finest talents. The play of the arms in the moderato and allegro in which the Maidens of Chalkis play at ball and knuckle bones by the seashore was also one of the effective bits.

The dances last night were in nowise different from those in which Miss Duncan has appeared in past seasons in this country and Europe, and her draperies were the same beautiful Greek arrangements. Repetitions of several of the dances were demanded by the large audience, and at the end of the programme Miss Duncan added several extra numbers concluding with *The Beautiful Blue Danube* waltz.

— *The New York Times*, November 10, 1909

1. Isadora Duncan first danced in New York as early as 1896, in Carnegie Hall Studio. After years in Europe, she next danced in New York in August, 1908 (Gluck's *Iphigenia*). Later she made a Continental tour and danced at the Metropolitan Opera House in December, 1908, then returning to Europe. This review in November, 1909, covers her second appearance in this theatre. / *Editor*

Miss Isadora Duncan again appeared at the Metropolitan Opera House yesterday afternoon and danced for the first time this season to Beethoven's A major symphony, which was played by the New York Symphony Orchestra, with Walter Damrosch conducting. It is quite within the province of the recorder of musical affairs to protest against this perverted use of the Seventh Symphony, a purpose which Beethoven certainly never had in mind when he wrote it. Because Wagner dubbed it the "apotheosis of the dance" is not sufficient reason why it should be danced to.

However, if one takes it for granted that Miss Duncan has a right to perform her dances to whatever music she chooses, there is no doubt of the high effect she achieves. Seldom has she been more poetical, more vivid in her expression of joy, more plastic in her poses, more rhythmical in her effects than she was yesterday. Wagner's title for the symphony might very properly be applied to Miss Duncan. As usual, she was most effective in the dances which require decisive movement. One of the wildest of her dances she closed with arms outstretched and head thrown back almost out of sight until she resembled the headless Nike of Samothrace.

The orchestra played Tschaikowsky's *Marche Slave*, a pantomime from Mozart's ballet music to *Les Petits Riens*, and a Beethoven *Polonaise* for the second part of the programme and then Miss Duncan danced five Chopin numbers. The audience was large and enthusiastic.

— *The New York Times*, November 17, 1909

Miss Isadora Duncan, the American girl who is directly responsible for a train of barefoot dancers who have spread themselves, like a craze, over two continents in the last five years, has returned to America, and yesterday she gave a new exhibition of her dancing, with the assistance of Walter Damrosch and the Symphony Society, at Carnegie Hall. Before the doors opened there were no seats to be had, and the long line of carriages which drew nigh the portals, as the hour set for the dancing to begin approached, indicated that Miss Duncan not only was the first of the barefoot dancers, but also the last. She not only has established her vogue, but she has also maintained it.

It has long been the custom for Miss Duncan to dance to music which originally belonged either to the opera house or the concert room. In years gone by she has lifted her feet to Chopin measures; to dances from the Gluck operas; and even to Beethoven's Seventh Symphony. This last was considered by many as a desecrating escapade, but many others paid money to see her do it, and Miss Duncan achieved some of her greatest popular success with the symphony which Wagner called the "apotheosis of the dance." Doubtless many people thereby became acquainted with a work of Beethoven which they never would have heard otherwise.

Yesterday Miss Duncan forsook the masters who have given her most of her material for dancing until now. She had arranged, in fact, an entirely new programme, through which to display her art. It was made up of excerpts from the Wagner music dramas and Bach's Suite in D.

If Bach did not intend that his music should be danced to, at least several of the numbers in this suite bear the names of dances, so Miss Duncan cannot be taken too much to task for employing them for her purposes.

The stage setting was what it usually is at a Duncan seance. Green curtains depended from the heights of the stage and fell in folds at the back and sides leaving a semi-circular floor in the centre on which dim rose-colored lights flitted here, contrasting with shadows there. When Mr. Damrosch came to the conductor's desk and raised his baton, all the lights in the auditorium were extinguished. The orchestra played the prelude to the suite and then Miss Duncan appeared.

She wore, as she always does, some drapery of diaphanous material. She stood for a moment in the shadow at the back of the stage while the orchestra began the *Air*, the celebrated slow movement in the suite, which violinists play on the G string. Miss Duncan waved her arms and posed during this movement but did not do much of what is conventionally called dancing.

In the two Gavottes and the Gigue which followed, however, the dancer was seen at her best. She flitted about the stage in her early Greek way and gave vivid imitations of what one may see on the spherical bodies of Greek vases. The Bourée from the suite the orchestra played alone and the first part of the programme closed with the Polacca from the first Brandenburg Concerto, also undanced.

There was a brief intermission before the Wagner excerpts were played. Then the house was darkened and the *Lohengrin* Prelude was performed. After this Miss Duncan gave her interpretation of the Flower Maidens' music from *Parsifal*.

This time she appeared in white gauze, beautifully draped. Her hair was caught up with flowers of pinkish hue. She evidently danced with an imaginary "Guileless Fool" standing in the centre of the stage. To him she appealed with all her gestures and all her postures. It was an interesting attempt to give the spirit of the scene in the Klingsor's garden. What it meant to those who have never heard Wagner's music drama this writer cannot profess to know.

The next number announced on the programme was the *Prelude* and *Liebestod* from *Tristan und Isolde*. Instead, however, of rapping for attention from his orchestra, Mr. Damrosch asked the audience for attention, turned about, and made a little speech.

The purport of his remarks was to the effect that it had originally been intended that Miss Duncan dance only music which had been arranged by Wagner in his music dramas for that purpose.

"It had been my intention," said Mr. Damrosch, "simply to play this music from *Tristan*. Yesterday, however, Miss Duncan modestly asked me if I would go through the *Liebestod* with her. She has, as is well known, a desire to unite dancing to music in a perfect whole, as an art which existed in the time of the early Greeks. Whatever she does now, of course, must be largely experimental. However, the results which she has already achieved with the *Liebestod* are so interesting that I think it only fair to set them before the public. As there are probably a great many people here to whom the idea of giving pantomimic expression to the *Liebestod* would be horrifying, I am putting it last on the programme, so that those who do not wish to see it may leave."

There was applause and then Miss Duncan gave her impressions of the Paris version of the Bacchanale from *Tannhäuser*, which were very pretty but hardly as bacchanalian as might have been expected. After the orchestra had played the Prelude to *Die Meistersinger* she danced the Dance of the Apprentices from that music drama. It may be stated that Miss Duncan did her best dancing of the afternoon to this number and it was repeated.

As for the *Liebestod*, the anticipation of it evidently was not too horrible for any one to bear. People did not leave their seats, except possibly the usual few who are obliged to catch trains. Miss Duncan's conception of the music did not seem to suggest a pantomimic Isolde, nor was it exactly dancing. In other words, she puzzled those who knew the music drama, and did not interest those who did not. Therefore one may ask, Why?

— *The New York Times*, February 16, 1911

It was to the operas of Gluck that Miss Isadora Duncan went for her first inspiration when she began her revivals of the Greek dance, and yesterday afternoon in Carnegie Hall she returned to Gluck. Her previous attempt to dance to the music from the lyric dramas of Richard Wagner had not resulted in complete success, but her spectators yesterday were pleased to see that Miss Duncan was herself again.

The first half of the programme consisted of copious excerpts from *Orfeo*, played in chronological order, and embracing the chief incidents of the book, with the exception of the scene in which Eurydice persuades Orpheus to turn and gaze upon her face. The Symphony Society of New York, Walter Damrosch conducting, played the music; a small chorus, seated among the orchestra, sang several of the choruses, and Mme. Florence Mulford sang several of Orpheus's airs.

In the first act, in a long robe of flowing gray, Miss Duncan represented one of the companions of Orpheus. Her poses and movements were intended to suggest the deepest grief. It was in the first scene of the second act, that of the scene in Hades, which was given in its entirety, that Miss Duncan, portraying one of the Furies, first aroused the enthusiasm of the audience. She indicated the gradual wavering of the Furies from the tremendous "No" in the beginning to the end when the Furies allow Orpheus to pass on to the Elysian Fields. The Dance of the Furies, with which this scene concludes, was a remarkable exhibition of dancing, evidence of high imagination.

It had originally been intended that several of the choruses and Orpheus's air from the scene of the Elysian Fields should be included in the programme scheme, but evidentally it was found necessary to omit these. Only the ballet airs were presented from this scene, including the famous air with flute obbligato, which was exquisitely played by Mr. Barrère.

Miss Duncan, as a Happy Spirit, was as much at home as she had been previously as a Fury. From here on a long excision was made in the score until the finale was reached; even the famous chaconne was omitted. In the final scene, in which the chorus again appeared, Miss Duncan indicated the triumph of Love.

The excerpts were beautifully played by Mr. Damrosch and his orchestra. It is worthy of note that the seldom heard overture, a usually omitted ballet air, and the finale, which is replaced at the Metropolitan Opera House by a finale from another opera of Gluck, were restored. As has been stated, much else was omitted.

After an intermission Miss Duncan danced to some music by Schubert, and the orchestra played Dvorak's *In The Spinning Room*.

— *The New York Times*, February 21, 1911

The New Isadora, 1917

I have a fine memory of a chance description flung off by some one at a dinner party in Paris; a picture of the youthful Isadora Duncan in her studio in New York developing her ideals through sheer will and preserving the contour of her feet by wearing carpet slippers. The latter detail stuck in my memory. It may or may not be true, but it could have been, *should* have been true. The incipient dancer keeping her feet pure for her coming marriage with her art is a subject for philosophic dissertation or for poetry. There are many poets who would have seized on this idea for an ode or even a sonnet, had it occurred to them. Oscar Wilde would have liked this excuse for a poem...even Robert Browning, who would have woven many moral strophes from this text...It would have furnished Mr. George Moore with material for another story of the volume called *Celibates*. Walter Pater might have dived into some very beautiful, but very conscious, prose with this theme as a spring-board. Huysmans would have found this suggestion sufficient inspiration for a romance the length of *Clarissa Harlowe*. You will remember that the author of *En Route* meditated writing a novel about a man who left his house to go to his office. Perceiving that his shoes have not been polished, he stops at a boot-black's and during the operation he reviews his affairs. The problem was to make 300 pages of this! . . . Lombroso would have added the detail to his long catalogue in *The Man of Genius* as another proof of the insanity of artists. Georges Feydeau would have found therein enough matter for a three-act farce and d'Annunzio for a poetic drama which he might have dedicated to "Isadora of the beautiful feet." Sermons might be preached from the text and many painters would touch the subject with reverence. Manet might have painted Isadora with one of the carpet slippers half depending from a bare, rosy-white foot.

There are many fables concerning the beginning of Isadora's career. One has it that the original dance in bare feet was an accident. . .Isadora was laving her feet in an upper chamber when her hostess begged her to dance for her other guests. Just as she was she descended and met with such approval that thenceforth her feet remained bare. This is a pretty tale, but it has not the fine ring of truth of the story of the carpet slippers. There had been barefoot dancers before Isadora; there had been, I venture to say, distinct "Greek dancers." Isadora's contribution to her art is spiritual; it is her feeling for the idea of the dance which isolates her from her contemporaries. Many have overlooked this essential fact in attempting to account for her obvious importance. Her imitators (and has any other interpretative artist ever had so many?) have purloined her costumes, her gestures, her steps; they have put the music of Beethoven and Schubert to new uses as she had done before them; they have unbound their hair and freed their feet; but the essence of her art, the spirit, they have left in her keeping; they could not well do otherwise.

Inspired perhaps by Greek phrases, by the superb collection of Greek vases in the old Pinakotheck in Munich,

Isadora cast the knowledge she had gleaned of the dancer's training from her. At least she forced it to be subservient to her new wishes. She flung aside her memory of the *entrechat* and the *pirouette*, she studied technique of the ballet; but in so doing she unveiled her own soul. She called her art the renaissance of the Greek ideal but there was something modern about it, pagan though it might be in quality. Always it was pure and sexless...always abstract emotion has guided her interpretations.

In the beginning she danced to the piano music of Chopin and Schubert. Eleven years ago I saw her in Munich in a program of Schubert impromptus and Chopin preludes and mazurkas. A year or two later she was dancing in Paris to the accompaniment of the Colonne Orchestra, a good deal of the music of Gluck's *Orfeo* and the very lovely dances from *Iphigénie en Aulide*. In these she remained faithful to her original ideal, the beauty of abstract movement, the rhythm of exquisite gesture. This was not sense echoing sound but rather a very delightful confusion of her own mood with that of the music.

So a new grace, a new freedom were added to the dance; in her later representations she has added a third quality, strength. Too, her immediate interpretations often suggest concrete images...A passionate patriotism for one of her adopted countries is at the root of her fiery miming of the *Marseillaise*, a patriotism apparently as deep-rooted, certainly as inflaming, as that which inspired Rachel in her recitation of this hymn during the Paris revolution of 1848. In times of civil or international conflagration the dancer, the actress, often play important rôles in world politics. Malvina Cavalazzi,[1] the Italian ballerina who appeared at the Academy of Music during the Eighties and who married Charles Mapleson, son of the impresario, once told me of a part she had played in the making of United Italy. During the Austrian invasion the Italian flag was *verboten*. One night, however, during a representation of opera in a town the name of which I have forgotten, Mme. Cavalazzi wore a costume of green and white, while her male companion wore red, so that in the *pas de deux* which concluded the ballet they formed automatically a semblance of the Italian banner. The audience was raised to a hysterical pitch of enthusiasm and rushed from the theatre in a violent mood, which resulted in an immediate encounter with the Austrians and their eventual expulsion from the city.

Isadora's pantomimic interpretation of the *Marseillaise*, given in New York before the United States had entered the world war, aroused as vehement and excited an expression of enthusiasm as it would be possible for an artist to awaken in our theatre today. The audience stood up and scarcely restrained their impatience to cheer. At the previous performances in Paris, I am told, the effect approached the incredible. . .In a robe the color of blood she stands enfolded; she sees the enemy advance; she feels the enemy as it grasps her by the throat; she kisses her flag; she tastes blood; she is all but crushed under the weight of the attack; and then she rises, triumphant, with the terrible cry, *Aux armes, citoyens*! Part of her effect is gained by gesture, part by the massing of her body, but the greater part by facial expression. In the anguished appeal she does not make a sound, beyond that made by the orchestra, but the hideous din of a hundred raucous voices seems to ring in our ears. We see Félicien Rops's *Vengeance* come to life; we see the *sans-culottes* following the carts of the aristocrats on the way to execution. . .and finally we see the superb calm, the majestic flowing strength of the Victory of Samothrace. . .At times, legs, arms, a leg or an arm, the throat, or the exposed breast assume an importance above that of the rest of the mass, suggesting the unfinished sculpture of Michael Angelo, an aposiopesis which, of course, served as Rodin's inspiration.

In the *Marche Slave* of Tschaikovsky, Isadora symbolizes her conception of the Russian moujik rising from slavery to freedom. With her hands bound behind her back, groping, stumbling, head bowed, knees bent, she struggles forward, clad only in a short red garment that barely covers her thighs. With furtive glances of extreme despair she peers above and ahead. When the strains of *God Save the Czar* are first heard in the orchestra she falls to her knees and you see the peasant shuddering under the blows of the knout. The picture is a tragic one, cumulative in its horrific details. Finally comes the moment of release and here Isadora makes one of her great effects. She does not spread her arms apart with a wide gesture. She brings them forward slowly and we observe with horror that they have practically forgotten how to move at all. They are crushed, these hands, crushed and bleeding after their long serfdom; they are not hands at all but claws, broken, twisted piteous claws! The expression of frightened, almost uncomprehending, joy with which Isadora concludes the march is another stroke of her vivid imaginative genius.

In her third number inspired by the Great War, the *Marche Lorraine* of Louis Ganne, in which is incorporated the celebrated *Chanson Lorraine*, Isadora with her pupils, symbolizes the gaiety of the martial spirit. It is the spirit of the cavalry riding gallantly with banners waving in the wind; the infantry marching to an inspired tune. There is nothing of the horror of war or revolution in this picture...only the brilliancy and dash of war...the power and the glory!

Of late years Isadora has danced (in the conventional meaning of the word) less and less. Since her performance at Carnegie Hall several years ago of the *Liebestod* from *Tristan*, which Walter Damrosch hailed as an extremely interesting experiment, she has attempted to express something more than the joy of melody and rhythm. Indeed on at least three occasions she has performed a Requiem at the Metropolitan Opera House...If the new art at its best is not dancing, neither is it wholly allied to the art of pantomime. It would seem, indeed, that Isadora is attempting to express something of the spirit of sculpture, perhaps what Vachel Lindsay describes as "moving sculpture." Her medium, of necessity, is still rhythmic gesture, but its development seems almost dream-like. More than the dance this new art partakes of the fluid and unending quality of music. Like any other new art it is not to be understood at first and I confess in the beginning it said nothing to me, but eventually I began to take pleasure in watching it. Now Isadora's poetic and imaginative interpretation of the symphonic interlude from César Franck's *Rédemption* is full of beauty and meaning to me and during the whole course of its performance the interpreter scarcely rises from her knees. The neck, the throat, the shoulders, the head and arms are her means of expression. I thought of Barbey d'Aurevily's phrase. "Elle avait l'air de monter vers Dieu les mains toutes pleines de bonnes oeuvres."[2]

Isadora's teaching has had its results for her influence has been wider in other directions. Fokine thanks her for the new Russian Ballet. She did indeed free the Russians from the conventions of the classic ballet and but for her it is doubtful if we should have seen *Scheherazade* and *Cléopatre, Daphnis et Chloë, Narcisse* and *l'Après-midi d'un Faune* bear her direct stamp. This then, aside from her own appearances, has been her great work. Of her celebrated school of dancing I cannot speak with so much enthusiasm. The defect in her method of teaching is her insistence (consciously or unconsciously) on herself as a model. The seven remaining girls of her school dance delightfully. They are, in addition, young and beautiful, but they are miniature Isadoras. They add nothing to her style; they make the same gestures; they take the same steps; they have almost, if not quite, acquired a semblance of her spirit. They vibrate with intention; they have force, but constantly they suggest just what they are. . .imitations. When they dance alone they often make a very charming but scarcely overpowering effect. When they dance with Isadora they are but a moving row of shadow shapes of Isadora that come and go. Her own presence suffices to make the effect they all make together. . .I have been told that when Isadora watches her girls dance she often weeps, for then and only then can she behold herself. One of the griefs of an actor or a dancer is that he can never see himself. This oversight of nature Isadora has to some extent overcome.

Those who like to see pretty dancing, pretty girls, pretty things in general will not find much pleasure in contemplating the art of Isadora. She is not pretty; her dancing is not pretty. She has been cast in nobler mould and it is her pleasure to climb higher mountains. Her gesture is titanic; her mood generally one of imperious grandeur. She has grown larger with the years — and by this I mean something more than the physical interpretation of the word, for she is indeed heroic in build. But this is the secret of her power and force. There is no suggestion of flabbiness about her and so she can impart to us the soul of the struggling moujik, the spirit of a nation, the figure on the prow of a Greek bark...And when she interprets the *Marseillaise* she seems indeed to feel the mighty moment. (*July 14, 1917*)

—From *The Merry-Go-Round*, Knopf, 1918

1. For more on the later career of Mme. Cavalazzi, see the section called "Metropolitan Opera Ballet" earlier in this volume. / *Editor*
2. (translation) She seemed to raise, towards God, her hands entirely filled with good works.

An Appreciation

Dear Walkowitz: I have examined your book of drawings of Isadora with great excitement. Again and again I found myself involuntarily exclaiming with the very phrases I formerly applied to the great dancer herself! It seems to me that you have successfully devoted a lifetime in an attempt to present to posterity the essence of Isadora Duncan. You have actually recreated her movement much more truly than a moving picture camera would have done. You give the precise feeling of her rhythm, the precision and intensity of her line, her flowing grace, and the massive proportions which served her to design nobility. You see her outside clearly because you understand what is within and work from the inside out. I think then that in this book of drawings of Isadora Duncan you have come as near as any artist could to completely analyzing and describing and reviewing the work of another artist in another medium.

Carl Van Vechten

—From *Isadora Duncan in Her Dances*, drawings by Abraham Walkowitz. Haldeman-Julius Publications, Girard, Kansas, 1945.

Maud Allan, 1910

Miss Maud Allan, an American girl, who has won no inconsiderable amount of fame in Europe and in England with her dances, made her initial appearance before a New York audience yesterday afternoon in Carnegie Hall. A large and very fashionable gathering greeted the dancer. In fact it has been a long time since so many automobiles have been lined up in front of this staid concert hall. Apparently all of the seats were filled and many were standing at the back. It was an enthusiastic audience, too, and Miss Allan was forced to repeat several of the dances which particularly caught the public fancy.

Most of Miss Allan's European reputation rests on a dance which she has called *A Vision Of Salome*, which introduces light and scenic effects, and which was one of the earliest symptoms of the later Salome craze which swept rapidly down from Germany across the Atlantic to New York, where it is just beginning to be brushed away.

It was not in this dance, however, that Miss Allan chose to make her first American appearance. Instead she elected to appear in another sort of dance with which New York is at present very familiar, thanks to Miss Isadora Duncan, the group of dancers which Miss Loie Fuller brought over, and finally to the ballet in Gluck's *Orfeo* as it is danced at present on the Metropolitan Opera House stage.

These dances, accomplished to music written by the great composers — it will be remembered that Miss Duncan even went so far as to use Beethoven's Seventh Symphony — exploit the dancer in poses presumably inspired by a study of Greek vases. Bare-limbed and scantily draped in filmy gauzes, diaphanous in texture and unvivid in color, she floats from one pose to the next, emphasizing the plastic transitions with waving arms and raised legs and sundry poses of the head.

Miss Allan in spirit and in the nature of her dances resembles her predecessors. However, she is more beautiful in fact and figure than some of them, and she has a grace, a picturesque personal quality, which is all her own. Yesterday the stage of Carnegie Hall was hung in green draperies and the lights but dimly indicated pale colors. The orchestra was the Russian Symphony Society, under the direction of Modest Altschuler.

It has been complained of in these columns that dancers take great liberties in dancing to music which was never intended for that purpose. However, Miss Allan in her programme yesterday scarcely transcended the bounds of good taste in this direction. She danced to Rubinstein's *Melody In F*, Mendelssohn's *Spring Song*, two mazurkas and a valse of Chopin, Grieg's *Peer Gynt* suite, the *Funeral March* from Chopin's B flat minor sonata, and Rubinstein's *Valse Caprice*.

—*The New York Times*, January 21, 1910

Miss Maud Allan, having launched herself at a previous New York matinee as a classical dancer, yesterday afternoon at Carnegie Hall presented herself in *The Vision Of*

Salome, the dance which made her name well known in London. This dance was devised by Miss Allan at the period when Oscar Wilde's play, Richard Strauss's music drama, and Franz von Stuck's pictures were creating the stir in Germany that they shortly afterward created in America. There is no record of Miss Allan having received any suitable recognition of her talents at that time, however. A little later, to be exact, in May 1907, she crossed the border line and appeared in Paris.

The Théâtre des Variétés was celebrating its one hundredth anniversary with a revue, much more splendid than those which are given in the ordinary Parisian music halls. This revue was nearing its seventieth performance, when the first rendering of Strauss's music drama *Salome*, in Paris, was announced at the Théâtre du Chatelet for May 8. Manager Samuel of the Variétés saw his chance. He brought out Miss Allan in *The Vision Of Salome* on the 7th. Her appearance at this theatre caused some discussion, but no sensation. That was reserved for her London appearance, which occurred some months later at the Palace Theatre. Since her début at this London music hall, Miss Allan's name has steadily grown in fame. For over a year in fact, she continued to do her nightly characterization of Salome in London.

Yesterday's representation differed in no marked respect from that of three years ago, and the stage setting was the same she had used in London. It is true that in Paris she had caressed the severed head of John the Baptist. Yesterday the head itself was left to the imagination but none of the caressing was. However, New York has seen so many dances of this sort by now that there were no exclamations of shocked surprise, no one fainted, and at the end there was no very definite applause.

Miss Allan's version of Salome presents a young girl who, having danced before Herod and asked for the head of John at the command of her mother, goes through the scene again in a dream. The stage is set to represent a garden of the palace, and in this garden Miss Allan yesterday executed steps and curved her body in contortions which are now conventionally supposed to suggest Salome.

Earlier in the afternoon Miss Allan danced to the *Peer Gynt* suite, a sarabande and gavotte of Bach's; Mendelsson's *Spring Song*, and Strauss's *Blue Danube*. All of these dances were accomplished in the prevalent classical manner and evoked much applause. The quality which Miss Allan possesses to a greater degree than her predecessors is a rhythmical sense.

The Russian Symphony Orchestra, under the direction of Modest Altschuler, played the accompaniments, and several other numbers. It should be appended for the sake of record that *The Vision Of Salome* was not accomplished to the dance music from Strauss's music drama, but to an "arrangement" possibly of Eastern airs, by Marcel Remey.

—*The New York Times*, January 30, 1910.

Loie Fuller, 1909

Miss Loie Fuller, known in Paris as La Loie, returned to dance in New York yesterday at the Metropolitan Opera House after several years's absence. Miss Fuller, it will be remembered, invented the serpentine dance, and devised light effects to simulate fire and other natural phenomena. It was in dances which employed manifold draperies and numberless colored lights that the dancer was formerly seen here. Since then, however, Isadora Duncan and Maud Allan have revived the Greek dance, at least their own ideas of the Greek dance, and Miss Fuller's performance yesterday afternoon included examples of these later-day conceptions as well as many of her own earlier creations.

For the first time that she has been seen here she was surrounded by a group of dancers, a complete ballet, in fact. Added to these were several solo dancers, many of whom have achieved Continental fame quite independently of Miss Fuller, but who have joined her company for this American tour. The programme, therefore, presented a varied aspect.

Miss Fuller and her muses were seen at the beginning in an interpretation of the Bach-Gounod *Ave Maria*. Following this, Orchidée, an American girl, who is young and beautiful, danced to a prelude of Chopin in Greek costume and with bare legs. Orchidée was later seen in a *Diana Dance*, which was most effective, and an interpretation of Mozart's *Turkish March*.

Mme. Thamara de Swirsky, a Russian dancer with quite another style but the same sort of costume, followed. Mme. Swirsky makes a more sensuous appeal than most dancers of the classic type. Miss Irene Sanden, a German girl, who is said to find her chief joy in dancing waltzes, followed in a waltz of Rubinstein and Strauss's *Roses From The South*.

The second part of the programme was in many ways the best half of the afternoon's entertainment. Miss Rita Sacchetto, who is well known in Europe, danced a dance of madness in Chopin's *Tarantelle*. The explanation of this dance is that a maiden who has been stung by a deadly spider can save her life only by mad dancing. The tempo increases with such intensity that the dancer breaks down, completely exhausted, only to rise again to intensified emotion.

Miss Sacchetto achieved a remarkably novel effect in this dance and succeeded in working the audience up to a high degree of enthusiasm. Many doubtless wished that they could see her perform her Spanish dances.

Miss Gertrude Van Axen, who shared this portion of the programme with Miss Sacchetto, was seen in Greek dances, into the scheme of which she fitted perfectly. Her figure is beautifully modeled and she is marvelously plastic.

The entertainment concluded with the Ballet of Light, in which the older ideas of Miss Fuller were incorporated and manifolded. If you have seen Miss Fuller perform her fire dance, in which the draperies take on the color and texture of flames, conceive of it as executed by thirty young women at once and you will have a picture of the Ballet of Light. Other dances of Miss Fuller's were manifolded in this same way, and the programme closed with the appearance of Miss Fuller herself.

A very large audience, which included many notable people, was in attendance, and the entertainment seemed to meet with approval. The Metropolitan Opera House orchestra, under the direction of Max Bendix, furnished the music.

— *The New York Times*, December 1, 1909.

The Negro Theatre

Editor's Note: Readers born since 1925 should bear in mind that at the time Van Vechten wrote the following article on the Negro theatre in 1919, the words "coon," "nigger," and certain references to the Negro dance which may seem crude and disrespectful to us, at the time of his writing were socially acceptable in Harlem as well as elsewhere. Carl Van Vechten, as much as any white writer, was sympathetic to and worked for the social improvement of the Black man's life in America. Any cursory investigation of his works and career supports this view.

When I was twenty-one the wonderful Williams and Walker Company was in full blast and bloom. The two comedians headed a large troupe of blacks and offered musical entertainment in a sense sophisticated but which did not dilute the essential charm, the primitive appeal of the Negro. There were reminiscences of the plantation, reminiscences of the old minstrel days, and capital portraits of the new coon, who was in those days a real figure and not a myth like the new woman, who as Agnes Repplier has pointed out in an amusing paper, has been in existence since the days of Eve. This organization must have travelled extensively, though I saw it only in Chicago, for I remember the posters which covered the South Side fencings and hoardings, picturing Williams and Walker appearing at Windsor, *by royal command* and Williams and Walker meeting Queen Victoria and the Prince of Wales. I am almost certain that one picture showed us the pair taking tea with royalty, but to this I cannot swear. These were the days of *Sons Of Ham* and *Abyssinia*. . . .

Bert Williams shuffled along in his hopeless way; always penniless, always the butt of fortune, and always human. He reblackened his face, enlarged his mouth, wore shoes which extended beyond the limits of even extraordinary feet, but he never transcended the precise lines of characterization. He was as definite as Mansfield, as subtle as Coquelin. Duse saw him on one of her American tours and promptly decided he was America's finest actor. His pantomimic powers were great and for their exploitation he relied almost entirely on his eyes and his hands, with the occasional aid of a bracing smile. In his poker game, for example, he developed a scene, without speaking a single word, which was enjoyable even to those spectators who did not play cards. To have heard him sing *I may be crazy but I ain't no fool, The phrenologist coon, All goin' out and nothin' comin' in* or the inimitable *Nobody* was to have heard and seen something as fine in its way as the contemporary theatre had to offer. Tobias Wormwood, Jasmine Jenkins, whatever character he assumed, left us trembling between hysterical laughter and sudden tears.

George Walker, on the other hand, the Rastus Johnson, the Harty Lafter, was the spick and span Negro, the last word in tailoring, the highest stepper in the smart coon world. How the fellow did prance in the cakewalk, throwing his chest and his buttocks out in opposite directions, until he resembled a pouter pigeon more than a human being! And we all shrieked applause until he had varied his walk nineteen times and repeated all the variations. As an Abyssinian monarch, breast, back, arms, and legs bare, a live bronze statue, Walker was a more barbaric figure, but even here his inclusive smile, which disclosed several glittering gold teeth, created a bond between Africa and Broadway. And his unction in *Bon Bon Buddy, the Chocolate Drop*! Supreme unction, I call it!...There were other features of these entertainments, Ada Overton Walker, for instance, who later became Aida, who danced as few white women have danced (the cry went, "Ain't she loose?") and who sang *I want to be a leading lady*. I can't recall these memories without crying. I feel very much the way William Winter must have felt when he thought of Edwin Booth. For George Walker is dead and so is his wife. Bert Williams drifted into the *Follies*, via vaudeville, but either the *Follies* or vaudeville killed him, for the Bert Williams of the *Follies* today is no more the Bert Williams of the Williams and Walker days than I am the Carl Van Vechten of 1898.

In December, 1913, there was a renaissance of the Negro theatre. I do not mean to say that between 1908 and 1913 no Negro companies appeared in our theatres; I do mean to say that no Negro company attracted my attention and my patronage. But in December, 1913, I learned (didn't everybody?) that a certain J. Leubrie Hill was appearing in a piece of his own concoction called *My Friend from Kentucky* with his organization known as the Darktown Follies at the Jefferson Theatre in the New York black belt.

This entertainment shared a fault common to all such enterprises, imitation of the white man's theatre. Mr. Hill evidently believed it necessary to add a dash of tenor, a sprinkling of girls in long satin gowns to his otherwise entirely fresh Negro salad. In due course these ingredients were stirred in. Then the actors on the stage singing conventional hymns to the moon, with accompanying action which Ned Wayburn might have devised, lost interest and the audience became listless and restless. But the greater part of the show was distinctly coon and the manner in which both entertainers and public entered into its spirit was again a great demonstration of a truth which is becoming more and more evident to those who work in the theatre that there must be complete co-operation between public and actor, that the audience indeed must become an integral part of any successful theatrical performance. The spectators at the Darktown Follies appeared to be enjoying themselves after the semi-hysterical fashion of a good camp-meeting. They rocked back and forth with low croons; they screamed with delight; they giggled intermittently; they waved their hands; they shrieked; and they pounded their palms vigorously together in an effort, which was availing, to make the entertainers work hard.

And the entertainers worked. They certainly did work. In *My friend from Kentucky* some attempt was made to present the Negro as he really is and not as he wants to be on the stage. The first act on a Virginia plantation diffused a general atmosphere of black joy. How the darkies danced, sang, and cavorted. Real nigger stuff, this, done with spontaneity and joy in the doing. A ballet in ebony and ivory and rose. Nine out of ten, nay ten out of ten, of those delightful niggers, those inexhaustible Ethiopians, those husky lanky blacks, those bronze bucks and yellow girls would have liked to have danced and sung like that every night of their lives and they showed it. How they stepped about and clapped their hands and "grew mad with their bodies," and grinned and shouted.

Then I saw the Congo:

". . .cake-walk princes in their long red coats,
Canes with a brilliant lacquer shine,
And tall silk hats that were red as wine.
And they pranced with their butterfly partners there,
Coal-black maidens with pearls in their hair,
Knee-skirts trimmed with the jessamine sweet,
And bells on their ankles and little black feet."

Passion and pleasure, pleasure and passion, a wholesome and tantalizing confusion, not at all like Spanish dancing but somehow suggestive at times of the primitive spirit of Spanish dancing.

In good Negro entertainment of this kind there is an inexorable rhythm, like the rhythm of a camp-meeting. Once under way it spreads from side to side of the stage. The separate figures become part of this great rhythm; the scenery and the stage boards take it up; the footlights flicker to it. J. Leubrie Hill reserved his great effort in this direction for the final scene of the piece in a number called *At The Ball* in which each entity of the company turned his body into that of a serpent, and then together they became one enormous serpent that coiled and recoiled all along its boneless and intolerable length. After the fiftieth repetition of this number the rhythm dominated me so completely that for days afterwards I subconsciously adapted whatever I was doing to its demands.

Night and after night Florenz Ziegfeld sat admiringly in a box at this show, drinking in the details of the admirable stage direction, the spontaneity of the performers, their characteristic lax ease, and the delightfully abandoned tunes. Several of these he bought, together with their accompanying action, and transplanted them into his *Follies Of 1914*, but the effect was not the same. The tunes remained pretty; the *Follies* girls undoubtedly were pretty, but the rhythm was gone, the thrill was lacking, the boom was inaudible, the Congo had disappeared.
(*February 3, 1919*)

— From "The Negro Theatre," *In The Garret*, Knopf, 1920.

The Lindy Hop

Every decade or so some Negro creates or discovers or

stumbles upon a new dance step which so completely strikes the fancy of his race that it spreads like water poured on blotting paper. Such dances are usually performed at first inside and outside of lowly cabins, on levees, or, in big cities, on street corners. Presently, quite automatically, they invade the more modest night-clubs where they are observed with interest by visiting entertainers, who, sometimes with important modifications, carry them to a higher low world. This process may require a period of two years or longer for its development. At just about this point the director of a Broadway revue in rehearsal, a hoofer, or even a Negro who puts on "routines" in the big musical shows, deciding that the dance is ready for white consumption, introduces it, frequently with the announcement that he has invented it. Nearly all the dancing now to be seen in our musical shows is of Negro origin, but both critics and public are so ignorant of this fact that the production of a new Negro revue is an excuse for the revival of the hoary old lament that it is pity the Negro can't create anything for himself, that he is obliged to imitate the white man's revues. This, in brief, has been the history of the Cake-Walk, the Bunny Hug, the Turkey Trot, the Charleston, and the Black Bottom. It will probably be the history of the Lindy Hop.

The Lindy Hop made its first official appearance in Harlem at a Negro Dance Marathon staged at Manhattan Casino some time in 1928. Executed with brilliant virtuosity by a pair of competitors in this exhibition, it was considered at the time a little too difficult to stand much chance of achieving popular success. The dance grew rapidly in favor, however, until a year later it was possible to observe an entire ballroom filled with couples devoting themselves to its celebration.

The Lindy Hop consists in a certain dislocation of the rhythm of the Fox Trot, followed by leaps and quivers, hops and jumps, eccentric flinging about of arms and legs, and contortions of the torso only fittingly to be described by the word epileptic. After the fundamental steps of the dance have been published, the performers may consider themselves at liberty to improvise, embroidering the traditional measures with startling variations, as a coloratura singer of the early nineteenth century would embellish the score of a Bellini opera with roulades, runs, and shakes.

To observe the Lindy Hop being performed at first induces gooseflesh, and second, intense excitement, akin to religious mania, for the dance is not of sexual derivation, nor does it incline its hierophants towards pleasures of the flesh. Rather it is the celebration of a rite in which glorification of self plays the principal part, a kind of terpsichorean megalomania. It is danced, to be sure, by couples, but the individuals who compose these couples barely touch each other, bodily speaking, during its performance, and each may dance alone, if he feels the urge or is impelled to by his partner. It is Dionysian, if you like, a dance to do honor to wine-drinking, but it is not erotic. Of all the dances originated by the American Negro, this the most nearly approaches the sensation of religious ecstasy. It could be danced, quite reasonably, and without alteration of tempo, to many passages in the *Sacre du Printemps* of Stravinsky, and the Lindy Hop would be as appropriate for the music, which depicts in tone the representation of certain pagan rites, as the music would be appropriate for the Lindy Hop.

—From *Parties*, pp. 183-185, Knopf, 1930

Nassau Dancing

...Like Negroes everywhere they sang a great deal, but I heard no folksongs. Rather they sang "Tipperary," or "Good-bye, boys, I'm going to be married tomorrow." I was amazed to hear one youth — he could have been no more than twelve — lustily whistling the "Marseillaise," with especial emphasis on those stirring phrases which underline the words, *Aux armes, citoyens!*

One night, on request, the natives arranged a "fire dance." This is a ceremony celebrated in secrecy during the season, when, according to report, the bucks and their doxies dance naked in some secluded nook in the forest, if a sufficient purse has been collected to make it worth their while. In the summer the young girls and boys prance for enjoyment before a bonfire, kindled for illumination rather than heat. They were quite willing to permit the spectacle to be observed, but the gate receipts apparently were not adequate to encourage disrobing. The music was furnished by a drum, made by fitting a skin over the head of an empty cask, and beaten with extraordinary rhythmic effect, and by the clapping of hands and singing of the group of native spectators. When the skin of the drum became loosened, it was held over the fire to dry taut again. The words of the songs were often indistinguishable; sometimes, indeed, they consisted merely of harsh cries. I can perhaps best designate their nature by appending a rude sample:

He's gwine roun' dah circle!
Tum ti tum tum, tum tum tum!
He's gwine roun' dah circle!
Tum ti tum tum, tum tum tum!

Monotonously, this primitive jingle was reiterated, until the dancers tired. The tunes did not vary greatly in effect, not at all in time, and they bore some esoteric, inexplicable relation to Russian folksong. As in so many of the Russian dances, one dancer performed at a time, indicating his successor by a nudge in his or her direction. There was not much variety in this exhibition, obviously, in its inception, symbolic of manifestations of sex. The movements included wild leaps, whirls, contortions of the body, girandoles, occasionally suggesting the barbaric Polovtsian dances in *Prince Igor*. Almost invariably, the arms were held close to the sides, sometimes with the forearm horizontal to the body, but seldom higher. A man advanced slowly, one leg dragging behind the other, with a curious

suggestion of lameness. One of the girls, a savage creature, with a mass of untutored hair, danced with a peculiar clawing motion of the hands. In one of her figures she stooped almost to the earth, continuing her odd rhythmic clawing as she shuffled around the circle of hand-clapping, shouting hysterics. Her thin arms and legs, her angular, awkward grace, if not her wild gestures, brought to mind the marionettes which are employed in Ceylonese shadow shows. When the crowd, excited, bent forward, encroaching too much on the central space, one of the boys snatched a fiery brand from the bonfire and with a swift sweep of his arm singed the bare feet of the eager spectators. They spread back with alacrity.
(*January 14, 1921*)

— From "On Visiting Fashionable Places Out of Season," pp. 14-16, in *Excavations,* Knopf, 1926.

Eloquent Alvin Ailey

The first important Negro dancing that I remember is George Walker's extravagantly elegant performance of the cakewalk, pranced with his equally talented wife, Aida Overton Walker, as partner; a performance derived from spectacular muscular control that, by comparison, makes other, more recent, exhibitions of this back-straining folk dance seem weak-jointed and flabby. George Walker could strut to the Queen's taste, and eventually, with his celebrated vis-à-vis, Bert Williams, he did just that at a command performance at Windsor Castle before the noble eyes of her Royal Majesty Queen Victoria, Empress of the Indies.

The next great Negro dancer I recall is Bill Robinson, the superb Bojangles, one of the few executors of any race who employed his entire body in his act. He tapped not only with his nimble feet, but also enlisted, with electrifying results, the aid of both hands, both expressive eyes, his mobile torso, and even his hat, which appeared to have a life of its own, in his brilliant exhibition.

After these major interpreters, Negro dancers arrived in profusion: Katherine Dunham, more a creator than a performer; Pearl Primus, who first developed a fine style all her own, moving expertly, with great precision to Negro folk tunes, and who later became adept in authentic African gyrations; Janet Collins, one of the earliest to create viable emotional movement for the spirituals, later enjoyed ending a program with a vivid impression of a tipsy New Orleans belle in red calico ruffles, returning from a Mardi Gras ball, and who eventually transformed — through her transcendent grace and magnetic personality — the ballet in the second act of *Aida* into a work of art on the vast stage of the Metropolitan Opera House. Avon Long was irresistible in his own sharply-etched, unique manner; Asadata Dafora was probably the first to introduce his native African dance to America; Josephine Baker, in her fantastic and capricious performances, aroused the jaded French to the highest degree of enthusiasm they had shown to any foreigner since the retirement of Mary Garden.

Arthur Mitchell has become an important artist with the New York City Ballet, and his partners are the most beloved of the white ballerinas. Mary Hinkson and Matt Turney are two of the most highly regarded dancers of the Martha Graham Company. Mary Hinkson has also danced with Arthur Mitchell and the New York City Ballet in *The Figure In The Carpet* and with Alvin Ailey in Harry Belafonte's *Sing, Man, Sing*.

I have seen the béguine danced to perfection at the Bal Colonial in Paris, and I have witnessed spectacular calypso dancing on the quai of Port of Spain, Trinidad, where Geoffrey Holder became acquainted with mystical voodoo rituals and the natural beauty of the West Indian folk dance.

Into the midst of this luxuriant medley, Alvin Ailey,

with his beautiful partner, Carmen de Lavallade (herself an unusually gifted dancer), plunged into *House Of Flowers* like two young animals. The effect was like that of a happy explosion. Such really desperate energy has rarely been evoked before in a light musical.

Alvin Ailey has all the attributes of a great dancer: he is young, beautiful, strong, with a perfect body and with the technique of dance well welded into his system. He knows how to approach practically all dance problems, except perhaps those of the classical ballet, and I dare say he could easily learn to perform these — given desire, time, and a period of study with the professional experience of George Balanchine. He can lift, leap, crawl and slide, even glide, to make your heart beat faster. His prodigious strength makes it possible for him to execute consecutive movements without pause in perfect rhythm. Great strength is the basis of all great dancing, for a dancer must be tireless in face of any difficulty. Ailey is a gifted actor, too, with real atmosphere in any costume he may assume.

Since her first appearance with him, Carmen de Lavallade has danced with him on many occasions, and they were seen together in their unforgettable brilliance in his low-down *Roots Of The Blues*, an experience — almost a career — for any beholder in its compelling realization of John Sellers' wailing melodies, illuminated by towering ladders in the background.

Alvin Ailey choreographs all the numbers he dances with skill, invention, a good deal of imagination, and variety. In the *Hermit Songs* of Samuel Barber, he employs a deeper, more passionate emotion than he used in *Roots Of The Blues* in his spontaneous and eloquent movement. He should further be inspected in *Revelations*, a dramatic setting of some familiar spirituals, and in *Gillespiana*, danced to music by the celebrated cornetist.

Some of us remember, many of us will never forget, a tender, introspective piece of Ailey's called *Ode And Homage*, in which he danced with a kind of solemn mournfulness. This was a tribute to his teacher, Lester

Horton, also the instructor of Janet Collins and Carmen de Lavallade. It was performed to music by Peggy Glanville-Hicks and was given only once in March of 1958. It can be said truthfully that it deserves a revival.

Alvin Ailey danced in Jamaica with Lena Horne's company, at Jacob's Pillow, at the Lewisohm Stadium, and in the picture version of *Carmen Jones*. He has also acted successfully in plays,. As a matter of fact, he is usually successful in whatever he attempts to do.

— From *Dance 62*. Copyright 1962 by Dance Perspectives, Inc.

Choreography For Americans

It is only of late years that the ballet has become a popular institution in the United States. It seems hard to believe, however, that less than thirty years ago there were empty seats at the Metropolitan Opera House when the great Nijinsky exhibited his peerless *brisés volés*. Even five years ago it was possible to buy good seats at the box office at eight o'clock the evening of practically any performance. But nowadays (1946, the war years, to define the period with exactitude) the great public, owing perhaps to increasing opportunity, has learned at least to enjoy the ballet. So much, indeed, that for several seasons the companies have found it profitable to give performances in hamlets as well as sizable towns, and to offer long seasons in New York in both the fall and the spring. In the approaching theatrical year we are promised a view of three such companies, possibly four. In addition, several star dancers will pirouette with their own "concert" groups to piano accompaniments, and practically every musical show will boast a ballet company of its own.

In the circumstances, a new guide to the intricacies of the art of dancing, providing American readers with some account of the dance plays currently exposed, was very much needed. In the past such volumes have usually been compiled with the English market in mind and when the Ballet Russe circulated freely between London and New York there could be no objection to this tendency as both repertory and dancers were familiar to spectators on either side of the Atlantic. The war and the birth of the Ballet Theater Company have changed all that. The Ballet Theater, a company organized in America in competition with the Ballet Russe de Monte Carlo, was obliged to build up, with the exception of the classical repertory, a new list of ballets of its own, and many of these have not yet been seen (or described) in England. Also the Ballet Russe de Monte Carlo, prevented by the war from leaving America, continued to add to its repertory. Both companies, of course, continued to develop new dancers.

London guide books then are practically bereft of information concerning the Antony Tudor ballets (Tudor's influence on the modern dance was beginning to be marked in London just as he left for America), and Agnes de Mille ballets, the Jerome Robbins ballets, the work of Eugene Loring, and the later Balanchine; nor can these books tell you anything at all about Nora Kaye, Alicia Alonso, Janet Reed, John Kriza and Harold Lang. Even Hugh Laing, perhaps the best young romantic male dancer the modern ballet has yet produced, has a reputation here which far transcends his London fame, for all his earlier seasons there.

It was to remedy this condition that Grace Robert has written her extremely readable *Borzoi Book Of Ballets,*[1] which not only covers the current repertory of the ballet companies presently touring America together with discussions and comparisons of the principal dancers, but also deals in extense with the classical repertory.

There is food for thought in the fact that *Giselle* has outlived all other ballets produced since her creation in 1841 and further that this mimed dance spectacle has never been absent from the stage for any extended period.

Additional evidence of the drawing power of the "white" ballet is to be extracted from the knowledge that *Les Sylphides* is the only one of Fokine's ballets to hold the stage consistently and continuously, while bits and pieces of the Tschaikovsky-Petipa ballet-repertory are the standbys and the war horses of all ballet companies, so that no season is held to be complete which doesn't award us glimpses (now in one act, now in another) of Odette-Odile, Aurora and the Sugarplum Fairy. Therefore, Mrs. Robert is well advised in giving these "white" ballets more extended attention, delving into the history of their productions and sketching descriptions of some of the more famous performers, paying hearty homage in passing to the great Markova, the dancer who decends in direct line from Taglioni and Pavlova, in some respects probably surpassing them both. Among present-day dancers, she is incomparable, and Mrs. Robert does not hesitate to say as much.

It is a pleasure to observe that, while the author in these pages expresses her opinions freely, for the most part it is not difficult to agree with her. I would, however, dissent when she dubs Eugene Loring's *Billy The Kid* the "finest ballet up to date on an American theme." Possibly the "first important American ballet" would be a more accurate description. Aaron Copland's music is always a delight, and the general conception of the choreographer is excellent, but certain scenes seem to be ineptly realized on the stage. Even the leading character does not come completely to life, while the role of the Mexican Sweetheart, particularly in her solo, seems impossible for any ballerina to deal with effectively. It is true that Agnes deMille's *Rodeo* owes something to *Billy The Kid*, but on the whole it is more skilfully conceived, more rounded out. Jerome Robbins's *Fancy Free* is a masterpiece from beginning to end, with no ifs, ands, or buts. I would even place *Interplay* ahead of *Billy The Kid* in entertainment value.

In a footnote on page nine of her book, Mrs. Robert goes out on a limb to observe that in a Russian movie short, "Bayaderka," Vachtang Chaboukiani displays a command of classic technique "that has never been seen in a New York ballet performance." This picture has not come my way, but I am wondering if Mrs. Robert may have forgotten that Nijinsky (not to speak of X, Y or Z) has danced in New York?

There are several omissions in the list of ballets described in this book, three, at least, of which are inexplicable: Agnes deMille's *Tally-Ho*, probably given as often on tour as any other item on the Ballet Theater list; Ruth Page's *Frankie And Johnnie*, and Jerome Robbins's *Interplay*. The omission of the latter is not particularly important as this ballet needs no exegesis. *Tally-Ho* in its original production did not quite come off, to be sure, but in the later performances Miss deMille was successfully aided by the interest Janet Reed gave to the principal role when she took it over, in bringing about something both distinguished and lusty. *Frankie And Johnnie*, too, with the fine performances it offers from Frederick Franklin, Ruthanna Boris, and Nikita Talin, is likely to retain its place for some time on the bills of the Ballet Russe de Monte Carlo.

On the positive side there is much more to be said for Mrs. Robert's book. The facts about each ballet are related simply and tersely without unnecessary padding. Usually the author gives us vivid descriptions of some of the performers, so that a reader in Oshkosh will be well fortified with knowledge about the cast he wants to see in any given ballet even before he has gazed, awe-struck, at a single variation. Further, this book is worth the price of admission for its discussion of all the important Tudor ballets, too recent to be included in past works of this character, although at present they form the backbone of the repertory of one of the best of the ballet companies. Mrs. Robert's review of *Pillar Of Fire*, for example, is as sympathic as the pages she devotes to *Pas de Quatre*, and the laurels she lays at the feet of the young American ballerina Nora Kaye are richly deserved. The book is illustrated, there is a glossary of balletic terms, and there is an index. It is no chore to read it. Any fully informed ballet-lover will find plenty to interest and delight him on almost any page, while the novice may acquire a considerable education painlessly.

— From "Weekly Book Review," p.7, in *New York Herald-Tribune,* Sunday, June 16, 1946

1. *Borzoi Book Of Ballets,* by Grace Robert. Knopf, 1946

Belief In An Ideal

While dining recently in a public restaurant with Christopher Isherwood, we were approached by an eager youth who proceeded to ask "literary" questions, firing them at us with alarming earnestness. We answered these as well as we could, but he hit upon that cliché, "Why do you write with a pen or on the typewriter? Why don't you dictate?" I knew how to answer directly and truthfully: "An author doesn't write with his mind, he writes with his hands." Isherwood, immediately struck by the validity of this statement, was also amazed by it. "Have you ever said or written that before," he demanded. I assured him that the remark was both spontaneous and pristine.

Reading Agnes de Mille's account of her career, *Dance To The Piper,*[1] I recalled this dictum and wondered why. Very speedily the reason was evident to me: Miss de Mille doesn't write or compose dances with her mind, she creates with her feet! I do not mean to imply by this statement that she is clumsy. Quite the contrary. I mean that whatever she has of genius flows from her soul into and through her feet.

I also recall a favorite theory of Theodore Dreiser's. He believed that if a man had talent or genius in one direction he could easily apply it in another direction. In other words, a writer should be able to compose or paint or walk on the ceiling for that matter, if he felt sufficient enthu-

49

siasm for the project. It was only a question of desire and of the *strength* of that desire.

Being a granddaughter of Henry George would seem to make it probable that Miss de Mille would be able to write, but *Dance To The Piper* is not very similar to *Progress And Poverty* in style or content. Nor does its author seem to have been influenced appreciably by her uncle, Cecil B. de Mille, or by her father, William de Mille.

Whatever and however, this dancer has written a great autobiography. I am familiar with the type of book usually negotiated by opera singers, actors, and ballet dancers. It is filled with sprightly or semi-tragic or sentimental anecdotes, for the most part unrelated to the general theme, and offering no illumination to it. The author may describe some character as a dancer, but we do not learn how or why she dances. Miss de Mille is not above anecdote. Indeed, this volume is rich in every variety. In each case, however, her use of anecdote is apposite, and adds something to the picture, the atmosphere, the story she is telling. Her powers of description are never idle or casual.

When, for example, she describes Martha Graham, she is not satisfied to call her great; she explains why she is great, why she is greater than her fellow artists: "Ballet has striven always to conceal effort; she on the contrary thought that effort was important since, in fact, effort was life. And because effort starts with the nerve centers, it follows that a technique developed from percussive impulses that flow through the body and the length of the arms and legs, as motion is sent through a whip, would have enormous nervous vitality. . . .She also evolved suspensions and falls utilizing the thigh and knees as a hinge on which to raise and lower the body to the floor, thus incorporating, for the first time, the ground into the gesture proper. All this differs radically from ballet movement. It is different from Wigman's technique, and it is probably the greatest addition to dance vocabulary made this century, comparable to the rules of perspective in painting, or the use of the thumb in keyboard playing. No dancer that I can name has expanded technique to a comparable degree. She has herself alone given us a new system of leverage, balance, and dynamics. It has gone into the idiom."

It will be observed from the above that this ballerina-choreographer, like her celebrated grandfather, knows how to think and is completely articulate. She is equally good at describing personalities. She is not afraid to underrate herself, and she has a devastating sense of humor. The form of this autobiography is based on the Cinderella legend. Once the success of *Oklahoma!* is attained and the Prince has discovered that the poor little rich girl is the owner of the glass slipper, the author drops her pen, leaving *Carousel, Allegro, Bloomer Girl, Tally-Ho, Fall River Legend, Brigadoon, Paint Your Wagon,* and the others to the imagination and maybe another book. Towards the end, as in a good ballet, *Dance To The Piper* gains in momentum, intricacy, and brilliance. The chapter on Marie Rambert completely reveals this remarkable woman, unknown in America. The chapters on *Rodeo* and *Oklahoma!* top the chapter on Marie Rambert. Indeed, I do not recall having read elsewhere such an authentic description of the glamour and horror of a dancer's life as is included in the *Rodeo* chapter. Does your daughter desire to become a dancer? If her enthusiasm is skimpy, give her this chapter to read, and she will discard her silly dream forthwith. On the other hand, if she has the real spark and is dedicated to the true vocation, if she reads this chapter nothing will persuade her to abandon her ambition.

Agnes de Mille's contention, the point of the book, its core and meaning, is that the young choreographers have developed a new form. "We had breached the bulwarks. Tudor, above all, then Ashton, De Valois, Eugene Loring, and I, lastly. Two years later Jerome Robbins with *Fancy Free* was to confirm the new tradition. (George Balanchine, whom many consider the greatest living ballet choreographer, was no revolutionist. He worked in the direct line of development from a classic premise.) How did we differ? We were trying to diversify the root impulse, and just as Gershwin impressed on the main line of musical development characteristics natural to his own unclassical environment, we were adding gestures and rhythms we had grown up with, using them seriously and without condescension for the first time. This is not a triviality. It is the seed and base of the whole choreographic organization. If dance gesture means anything, it means the life behind the movement."

Miss de Mille struggled hard to attain these ends, and in this book she fully exposes that struggle, the pain it caused her and others, without skipping a bad temper, a tired muscle, or a sleepless eye. But nobody can read this history of courage and belief in an ideal without understanding both dancing and human nature a little better. Indeed, I believe nobody can read this book without following it up with a salutation, "Bravo, Agnes de Mille!"

— "Belief in an Ideal," January 26, 1952 *The Saturday Review.*

1. *Dance to the Piper*, by Agnes de Mille. Little, Brown, 1952.

Terpsichore and The U.S. Army

A dancer who is at once literate and articulate may be considered a novelty, and probably Agnes de Mille is unique in this department. It is true, certainly, that other dancers have written books, mostly on their chosen vocation, but Miss de Mille has given evidence that she could write in any formal plan that she selected as desirable. The present example, indeed, might have been a novel, as it is assuredly a love story.

The author has always been enamored of the ballet and of dancing in general, and she writes superbly about other dancers, of whom she has introduced quite a few (among others, Diana Adams, Annabelle Lyon, Pearl Lang, Joan

McCracken, Sono Osato, Gemze de Lappe, James Mitchell, John Butler, Peter Birch, Marc Platt, and Kay Kendall). Moreover, she has had an excellent education and knows the history of the world of Terpsichore thoroughly. Dancing is discussed concretely and at great length in *And Promenade Home*[1] and there are at least two excellent chapters devoted to an abstract discussion of the art.

Possessed of a natural affinity for writing, Miss De Mille expresses herself with elegance, with eloquence, and with clarity. She is intimate with the intricacies of the English language and can communicate with an expert subtlety that frequently verges on brilliancy. She is at home describing the attitudes and movements of the dance, and she is equally *chez elle* when she describes her friends. She has humor and even knows how to laugh at herself — on occasion a suitable subject for laughter. She can be brutally frank, even about herself, but when her frankness is applied to others it seems to be doubly frank. It is possible, now and again, that she overpraises her pets, but she is considerably less emphatic in condemnation. On the whole, she is generous and fair in her judgements, which occur on every page — and she is seldom dubious when expressing an opinion.

In the first volume of her autobiography, *Dance To The Piper*, Miss de Mille recorded her initial failures at some length, describing a bleak period when no one except herself and her mother had any real conception of what she proposed to do. In the present book she briefly summarizes these early years, not without tears, but before long she plunges into a description of her choreography in *Oklahoma!*, a work — still alive nine years after its creation — which completely changed the role of dancing in subsequent musicals and which elevated Agnes de Mille to an important position in the theatre world. There also is a record of her further brilliant progress, through *One Touch Of Venus, Rodeo, Tally-Ho, Carousel, Brigadoon,* etc. Miss de Mille's work on these productions is tenderly described in detail (but sometimes the detail is unpleasant). There is no mention of *Three Virgins And A Devil*, in which Jerome Robbins made his debut in a principal part, or of another piece or two designed by our Lady Tinkletoes.

Actually, this book is mostly concerned with Walter Prude, now her husband, whom she meets (on page 14) through the auspices of Martha Graham, and whose baby she is preparing to bear towards the close of the volume. Their separations are maddening, sometimes the result of orders from his superiors, sometimes caused by her stupidity. At any rate, the book is about Lieutenant Walter F. Prude, United States Army, and her relations with him, and her feelings about him, and her reactions of *his* feelings about *her*. So intimately and realistically are these emotions expressed that a sympathetic reader, believing reasonably enough that he is reading fiction, will be moved as he would be by the emotional text of a novel. Very occasionally, with a good deal of trepidation, she asks Walter Prude to see her ballets, and it is worthy of comment that the reader never does discover what he thinks about them.

It is not remarkable then to learn that even the chapters devoted to the ballet are in a not-too-mysterious way tangled with her feelings for her husband. This is most evident in a chapter about the Civil War ballet in *Bloomer Girl* when all the upper theatre brass was against her. E.Y. Harburg, John C. Wilson, and even Main Bocher (who had been called in to referee) begged her to scrap this ballet as too serious for a lighthearted musical. She was obdurate: war to her was a serious business. Only Trude Rittman and the dancers were with her, but *how* they were with her! Standing her ground, without yielding an inch, she enjoyed her first triumph on the opening night when the opposition were on their knees before her.

In the chapter entitled "The Milk Of Paradise," Miss de Mille turns over in her mind and heart her attitude toward her husband; she wonders if his return will be sufficient compensation for her long extended loneliness and will make it possible for her to retire as a choreographer, to rest content in his arms. She learns that the answer is No, that she will continue to love her husband, but that she will also continue with her work. At this point she quotes Maurice Goudeket, husband of Colette, who has written: "A man does not love a woman for her genius; he loves her in spite of her genius." And Miss de Mille reflects on woman's lot since the beginning of time, how her talents have always been held down by the Church, by the Family, and by Man in general. She considers the rewards that may come to her as a great choreographer, she considers her unusually complete preparation for such a role, and she determines to carry on.

There is another chapter about the ballet which makes grimmer reading, but which is even more affecting because it is more general in application. Miss de Mille explains why the steps in choreography, the whole plan of any particular ballet, can be stolen and utilized in a subsequent and inferior production without payment to the original choreographer, who has no redress in the face of these shameful circumstances. Dance movements can hardly be set down intelligibly. There is a system of accurate dance notation, but no dancer can read it. Certainly, as yet, no Congressman can read it. She explains in detail a choreographer's job, how he (or she) is engaged to create dances for a certain space of time in a musical show, as necessary and valuable to the piece as any other detail. Furthermore, he is frequently given no hint of the kind of steps and movements that are needed. Sometimes even the music for the ballets is not ready. In spite of this, the choreographers' attempts to convince Congress that this kind of work should be protected by law have been consistently unsuccessful.

"At this writing (asserts Miss de Mille) the situation is considerably worse. Producers and managers are aroused by choreographers' growing demands. Authors go to particular pains to write dancing out of the shows or to keep it well corralled in unimportant little corners. Rank beginners are brought in at bottom prices. There is a very real rivalry between directors and choreographers for power, prestige, and percentages. Jerome Robbins and Michael Kidd have solved matters by organizing, directing, producing, and choreographing their own shows. This is a heroic answer and one not possible for many. There could be another: simple justice."

— "Terpsichore and the U.S. Army," October 18, 1958 *The Saturday Review*.

1. *And Promenade Home,* by Agnes de Mille. Little, Brown, 1958.

2

Russians

*"Russians are natural dancers...
Nijinsky... the greatest of stage artists...
(his) element is the air...
one can only compare him with himself."*

Secret of the Russian Ballet

Irony certainly directed the workings of fate when it was decreed, in this age of individualism, that the group-spirit should dominate the movements of the theatre, an institution in which, not so many years ago, the individual reigned, his head crowned with bays. Democracy has two effects: it strengthens the individual and it gives him the power to join with other individuals in fostering the growth of his ideals. Thus Max Reinhardt, distinctly individual though he may be, has made his impression through his artists, his actors, and his musicians. So has Stanislawsky of Moscow, who in one instance solicited the services of Gordon Craig. The Irish Theatre movement, which developed so great a genius as Synge and many lesser, but still important, writers, such as T.C. Murray and St. John Ervine, was essentially conceived in the group-spirit. But more than any of these, the most brilliant movement in the theatre of our time, the Russian Ballet (I am referring specifically to the organization under the direction of Serge de Diaghilew) has relied to an extraordinary degree on the group for its effect — one which, on modern art, music, dancing, stage decorations, and women's fashions, can scarcely be overestimated. I have heard it said, not altogether as a jest, that the Russian Ballet has had an influence on European politics.

There are still many people, however, who have never seen the performances of the Russian Ballet, who think of it only as an aggregation of virtuosi, much after the manner of one of Mr. Grau's all-star casts in *Les Huguenots*. It is true that the names of Nijinsky, Karsavina, Fokine, Massine, Bolm, and Fokina have inevitably awakened the same sort of magic sympathy that the names of Nordica, Melba, Calvé and the de Rezskes once evoked. The misunderstanding has followed in natural sequence. Nevertheless — and this is said without any desire to depreciate the value of the Russian stars — it is fortunate that the ideal of the producers of these mimed dramas is aimed higher than at the exploitation of individual talent. Their ultimate goals are cohesiveness and general pictorial effect. And this fact makes it possible for the Ballet to give representative performances with or without the aid of any particular dancer. In the summer of 1914, for example, in the absence of the superlative Nijinsky, the Russians made very lovely productions of Rimsky-Korsakow's *The Golden Cock* and Richard Strauss's *The Legend of Joseph*.

For any comprehensive view of the achievements of the organization, it is essential to remember that Mr. de Diaghilew's Russian Ballet began in Paris as an art exhibition; that is the secret. For two seasons Bakst and other Russian painters hung their pictures in the French capital. These two picture-shows are now included in the official lists of the Russian Ballet seasons, and by no means accidentally, or for purposes of misrepresentation. For the ballet has, in a large sense, continued to be a picture-exhibition, and in spite of the fact that some of the novelty has been worn off by multiplied imitations, the thing itself still retains a good deal of the original impulse. The Russian Ballet, on its decorative side, is entirely responsible for the riot of color which has spread over the Western world in clothes and house furnishings. Without the Russian Ballet as an inspiration there could have been no Paul Poiret, no Paul Iribe, no George Barbier, no Jean Cocteau, no George Lepape, no Marcel Lejeune. There surely would have been no "Gazette de Bon-Ton" and no department-shop sales of striped and spotted fabrics of every shade under the sun. George Bernard Shaw did not stretch the truth when he said that for the past five years the Russian Ballet has furnished the sole inspiration for fashions in women's dress...One does not need to remember any further back than the summer of 1914, when *Papillons* and *The Legend of Joseph* were produced, to follow him. The crinolined ruffled skirts of the former ballet and the prim Veronese gowns of the latter (recall Lillah McCarthy's dresses in *The Doctor's Dilemma*) have been repeated in a thousand forms. And so we might go back, year by year, to the season when Bakst's *Sheherazade* launched the Oriental craze which is still making itself felt in hamlets on the Great Lakes.

These decorations, and the costumes which accompany them, designed by such artists — many of them well-known painters in Russia — as Roerich, Bakst, Fedorowsky, Soudeikine, Golovine, Doboujinsky, Alexander Benois, and Nathalie Gontcharowa, are the basis of the beauty of the Russian Ballet, and they are so perfect in their many manifestations that no amount of imitation can entirely spoil them. When Roerich's scene for the Polovtsian camp in *Prince Igor*, a composition in dull greys and reds, with low, round-topped tents and rising columns of smoke, was disclosed in Paris, Jacques Blanche, the French painter, was moved to write an article in which he hailed the designer as the inventor of a new type of stage scenery, and even called upon the easel painters to learn a lesson in truth from this rugged Russian. Roerich subsequently designed the very beautiful green landscape for the first scene for Strawinsky's *The Sacrifice to the Spring*, and the grewsome setting, between somewhere and nowhere, of the second. To Fedorowsky are due the barbaric decorations and costumes for Moussorgsky's opera, *La Khovanchina*. The dresses of the Persian ballet in this opera, orange riots, speckled with patches of deep green and blue, have been plentifully imitated. Soudeikine devised the extravagant ostrich-plumed gauds worn by the six negroes who accompanied Florent Schmitt's Salome on her decadent way. And Nathalie Gontcharova, with exquisite fantasy, designed the scenes and costumes for *The Golden Cock*, a production in which the Russians showed that they were willing to go yet further in the realms of color-combination than they had before ventured. Bakst, of course, is as well known to us as Aubrey Beardsley or Longfellow. There have been books of his work on sale; the magazines and newspapers have reprinted many of his designs; there has been an exhibition of his original drawings at the Berlin Photographic Galleries in New York. However, in spite of the reproductions and imitations, I think those who have not yet seen a Bakst production, such as *Sheherazade, Daphnis et Chloë,* or the extraordinary *Legend of Joseph,* on the stage, may prepare for a thrill.

The scene exposed on the very large Drury Lane stage as the curtain rose on Richard Strauss's ballet was certainly very splendid in its majestic beauty. The stage directions give some conception of the picture:

"The scene, the stage furniture, and the costumes are throughout in the manner of Paolo Veronese, and thus follow, in style and fashion, those of the period of about 1530. The Egyptian characters wear Venetian costumes; Joseph and the dealers who bring him to Potiphar, Oriental dress of the sixteenth century. The scene represents a huge pillared hall in the Palladian style. The pillars and ceiling are of bright gold with a greenish sheen. The floor is inlaid with blocks of colored marble. The background is traversed by a raised loggia, also of gold, which is open to the air on the farther side, and gives a view over gardens with playing fountains, and distant wings of the palace; the openings on the further side are, however, curtained during the banquet by a vast carpet of Flemish work representing the Earthly Paradise — stretches of verdure, alive with exotic beasts of every kind. The loggia has no balustrade, but is open between the pillars from floor to ceiling, so that the personages traversing it are entirely visible from head to foot. On the right a flight of steps leads up to the loggia. Over the floor of the loggia an Oriental carpet is hung, reaching down to the hall.

"On the stage in front of the loggia are set two tables at right angles to each other; the one furthest from the spectator is rather long and runs parallel to the supporting wall of the loggia; the other is only short, and joins the first at right angles on the left. The table to the front is raised on three steps as a dais. On the tables are richly chiselled vessels of gold and silver, high ewers of cut crystal full to the brim with gleaming red and white wines, and dishes in which lie, heaped in profusion, pomegranates, peaches, and grapes of unusual size: golden platters and crystal glasses are before the guests. The guests — men and women by threes, in opulent Venetian costumes — sit at the farthermost side of the table at the back, half concealed behind the vessels of gold, the crystal, and the piled fruit. At the table in front Potiphar and his wife, the latter in a robe of scarlet brocade, cut very low, over which hang long strings of pearls. At her feet on the lowest step of the dais, a young female slave. The tables are served by eight negro slaves in a semi-Oriental garb of pink and gold, and on their heads are nodding plumes of white and pink. Behind the dais, in the angles to the left, under the loggia, Potiphar's bodyguard — gigantic mulattos, with breastplates of black inlaid with gold, of Toledo workmanship, with black plumes and halberds of gold. They also carry whips with short golden handles."

The spaciousness of this picture, the sense of splendor it conveyed, cannot be communicated second-hand. A young Spanish painter, José-Maria Sert, designed the majestic loggia, and Bakst vivified the scene, truly Veronese, with its women in gorgeous brocades, flaring skirts, puffed sleeves, and stilted mules, the officers in waving plumes, two of the slaves holding lank greyhounds in check. One detail was essentially Bakst. In the old Venetian costumes a panel of lace, down the front, covered the opening made by the flaring brocades. This Bakst removed, exposing the legs of his women, in silken hose, tightly trousered above the knee. This undergarmenting, in its inception, is authentic, as anyone may see who visits the Museo Civico Correr in Venice.

I have hesitated this long over *The Legend of Joseph* because, in reproduction at least, it is one of the least familiar of the Bakst ballets, not because it is more interesting than *Sheherazade, Daphnis et Chloë,* or a half-dozen others of this artist's productions.

In considering the factors which go to make up the perfection of this organization it is necessary to lay considerable stress on the importance of the music. In each of the cities where the Ballet has appeared a large orchestra of picked musicians (in some instances an organized orchestra, such as Thomas Beecham's in London) has assisted at the performances. The music of the ballets, even when adopted for this use, as in *Cléopâtre,* is of a fine quality, and in the variety of the compositions employed (ordinarily three or four ballets make up a programme) and in the manner of their performance there is the greatest amount of interest for those who are more interested in hearing than in seeing. Particularly is this true as the Russian Ballet has been the means of bringing some of the most radical and anarchistic of modern composers to a hearing before the public. Since Tschaikowsky wrote three ballets, no musician in Russia has considered it less than an honor to write for dancing.

Certain of the works performed have been taken from the concert room, *l'Après-midi d'un Faune,* for example, with the approval, and even the applause, of Monsieur Debussy; and *Sheherazade,* in spite of the protests of Rimsky-Korsakow's heirs. Balakirew's *Thamar,* too, was programme music before it became a ballet. But several works have been written for performance by this organization. Among these I may mention Maurice Ravel's *Daphnis et Chloë,* the music of which exactly illustrates the action of the ballet but is not easily transferable to the concert room, although Ravel made an arrangement which the Colonne Orchestra has played in Paris and the Symphony Society of New York has performed in New York; Debussy's *Jeux;* Reynaldo Hahn's *Le Dieu Bleu;* Steinberg's *Midas;* Tcherepnine's *Narcisse;* Richard Strauss's *The Legend of Joseph,* which the composer himself conducted for several performances both in London and in Paris; and the three really extraordinary works of Igor Strawinsky, *The Firebird, Petrouchka,* and *The Sacrifice to the Spring.* I have elsewhere expressed my great admiration for the genius of this young man;[1] it is certainly my opinion that more inspiration is made manifest in these three works than in any other recent music I have heard in the theatre or the concert room. Paul Dukas also wrote a ballet for the Russians, *La Péri,* but although it was announced, the production was finally made under other auspices.

Any concert-goer will immediately note the fact that a good deal of the music in the répertoire of the Russian Ballet is familiar to him. Balakirew began his symphonic poem, *Tamara* (the ballet is called *Thamar*), suggested by a poem by Lermontoff, in 1867; it was concluded in 1882. The composer wrote in 1869 that he had composed parts of it as he "danced along" the street. The Chicago Orchestra performed the work for the first time in America in 1896. The Russian Symphony Society introduced it to New York in 1908. When the Russians adopted the work to use as a ballet the critic of the "Morning Times" in London said that the action did not fit the music very well, and yet the story of the ballet is almost precisely that of the symphonic poem, so that if anyone was at fault in this regard it must have been the composer. Here is the fable to which Balakirew wrote music, in the words of the programme notes (by William Hubbard Harris) of the Chicago Orchestra:

"In the narrow Dariel Pass, where the River Terek roars, covered with heavy mists, there rises an ancient tower, in which there lived Queen Thamar, an angel of beauty, a cruel, wily demon in thoughts, and yet at the same time divine. At her enchanting call the passing traveller entered the tower to take part in the banquet in progress there. Shouts and cries of revelry awakened echoes in the darkness, as if at a great feast a hundred young, pleasure-loving men and women were gathered, or as if, in that great tower, erstwhile forbidding, the celebration of funeral rites were taking place. At the break of day gloomy silence again reigned, broken only by the foaming Terek as it hurried away a corpse. At this moment there appeared at the window a pale shadow. It waved afar a last farewell to the loved one. That farewell breathed such tender ecstasy, the voice which uttered it was so sweet, that its every accent, filled with promise, seemed to tell of near, unspeakable happiness."

Only in its conclusion does the ballet action vary from this story. The Queen lures the Prince to his doom, dances with him as the centre of a bacchanale, and then gives him the knife-thrust, as her slaves hurl him through an opened door into the river. But as the curtain falls we see her, not waving farewell to her old victim, but waving welcome to a new one.

Perhaps the composer really was at fault, because the music has never made a profound impression in this country. Here is W.J. Henderson's account of it in "The Sun," following the performance by the Russian Symphony Society:

"Tamara was a queen, and she dwelt by the River Terek in an ancient tower, where she was wont to indulge in nights *à la Cléopâtre russe*. In the mornings the dead bodies of her lovers went floating down the stream, while she sang exquisite love-songs, just as if her lovers could be lured back. In the music of Balakirew one could hear the river, which sounded much like the Rhine, even to suggestions of the Drachenfels. The riotous nights were perhaps less clearly indicated. They were somewhat repressed, muffled, as it were. Perhaps Tamara, out of consideration for the neighbors, used to shut the windows when she was holding high jinks on the banks of the blue Terek in the Caucasus. But they had long nights up there, for the listener sitting outside the tower (in a hard orchestra chair) and waiting for the exquisite love-song, grew stiff and cold. And, after all, it was a mean little love-song, because it had no tune, and it would not have lured a red-headed boy, let alone a dead man."

However, Mr. Henderson had not seen Karsavina as the wicked queen when he wrote those lines, nor had he seen Bakst's gorgeous Georgian costumes — a variant, it is true, of the greens and blues with which he had decorated *Sheherazade*. The fault of the ballet, as a whole, is that it is reminiscent of *Sheherazade*; and yet it is effective and has persisted in the répertoire of the Russians since it was first given in 1912. The overdresses of the women gave rise to one of the fashions in women's gowns which spread over our world two years ago.

Rimsky-Korsakow's *Sheherazade* is another matter. The music was not written to accompany the story used in the ballet, and yet it fits it perfectly. Still, Mme. Rimsky-Korsakow (the composer, of course, is dead) protested violently against what she called a desecration of her husband's intention, when the ballet was first produced. (A similar protest was lodged against the organization in 1914, when it produced Rimsky-Korsakow's last opera, *The Golden Cock,* with a double cast, one choreographic and one vocal, although the opera had been written to be *sung.*) No piece of music is better known in the concert hall than this, and any concert-goer will remember the violin theme which portrays the last of the Sultan's wives, as she relates the four stories from the "Arabian Nights" which the four movements of the Suite describe. The ballet follows the action of the prologue of these stories; the women of the harem steal the keys from the grand eunuch and let loose the black slaves for a drunken revel of lust, which is interrupted by the sudden return of the sultan and death to all concerned. The third movement, that which in the Suite describes the love of the young prince and the young princess, was omitted from Fokine's original arrangement of the ballet, but in 1914 he added this movement to the action. *Sheherazade* has been considered since the time it was first produced in Paris some six years ago, the masterpiece of the Russians. It made the designer of its scenery and costumes, Leon Bakst, famous. His color-scheme, mostly of greens, blues, and oranges, has been frequently imitated in later theatrical productions. Karsavina's Zobeide is a suggestive picture of languorous lust, and Nijinsky, as the principal slave, alternates between surprising leaps into the air and the most lascivious gestures, as, like some animal, he paws the reclining Sultana.

L'Après-midi d'un Faune is as well known as *Sheherazade* in the concert room. This was the first ballet which

Nijinsky staged (he also enacted the principal rôle). The music was written by Debussy as a prelude to Mallarmé's somewhat obscure poem. An English translation, at least an acceptable one, has hitherto been lacking, but Walter Conrad Arensberg's very sympathetic and understanding version has just appeared; were it not for its length I should like to transcribe it here. When Debussy's work is performed Edmund Gosse's summary of his idea of the meaning of the poem (with which, by the way, the poet expressed himself as entirely pleased) usually appears in the programme notes. But Debussy's music is called a *prélude* to the poem and so the action of the ballet is a prelude to the wonderings of Mallarme's faun. This is the scenario as it was printed in the programmes given out for the first Paris performances:

"Ce n'est pas *l'Après-midi d'un Faune* de Stéphane Mallarmé; c'est, sur le prélude musical à cet épisode panique, une courte scène qui la précède:

"Un Faune sommeille;

"Des Nymphes le dupent;

"Une écharpe oubiée satisfait son rêve.

"Le rideau baisse pour que le poème commence dans toutes les mémoires."[2]

There are, I think, seven nymphs engaged in the performance. Their dresses and their action are suggestive of the figures of Greek vases and bas-reliefs. One after another they flee from the strangely misunderstanding faun, until one, bolder than the others, approaches, almost to remain. The faun still does not understand and she, too, flees, dropping her scarf behind her. This the faun seizes and, as the curtain descends, returning to his rock, he presses this scarf to his lips and breast, at last, apparently something more than the faun he has been. Nijinsky in this pantomine (it can scarcely be called a ballet) suggests all that the poem and the music call forth in imaginative minds. He has dehumanized the characters and, in a sense, thereby taken away the sting of the too intense voluptuousness of the action. However, in spite of this fact, and the further one that Monsieur Debussy, unlike Mme. Rimsky-Korsakow, not only approved of the use of his music in this form but even applauded it, the first performance in Paris (1912) was roundly hissed. Paul Souday, a well-known critic, led the opposition, and Rodin took up the cudgels for the defence. "Accusé d'avoir 'offensé le morale,' Nijinsky s'est empressé de donner satisfaction à M. Paul Souday en supprimant sa 'mimique indécente' à la fin du ballet. Et pourtant, son illusoire possession de la nymphe enfuiée, ce corps étendu sur le voile encore parfumé d'elle, c'était beau!" wrote Gauthier-Villars.[3] It is true that Nijinsky altered his original performance for a few evenings; then, however, he returned to his original conception. Meanwhile, the troup moved to London, where *l'Après-midi d'un Faune* was acclaimed above all the other ballets, and almost invariably *repeated.* Since then it has seldom been given in London and Paris without the audience demanding a repetition.

Les Sylphides, Papillons, Carnaval, and *Le Spectre de la Rose,* are all exquisite studies of a different style from the three ballets I have mentioned. *Carnaval* is undoubtedly the best of the lot, although Nijinsky as the rose ghost (the fable was suggested by a poem of Théophile Gautier) who comes to a young girl in a dream and bounds out of the window, like a spirit, at dawn, is in his most poetical mood. *Papillons* is the newest of these four ballets, and for it Bakst designed some charming crinolined dresses. Pierrot, in the garden, after the dance, has set a candle to catch butterflies, and as the dancers flit out, each pretending to be a butterfly, he tries to catch them, until the coming of their parents to take them home teaches him the bitter truth that they are only young girls. The music is by Schumann, orchestrated by Tcherepnine. *Les Sylphides* is little more than a suite of dances in a charming adaptation by Bakst of the conventional ballet costume. Glazunow and other Russian composers have orchestrated these Chopin waltzes, mazurkas and preludes. In *Carnaval* (orchestrated by Tcherepnine, Glazunow, Liadow, and Rimsky-

Korsakow) the fanciful names by which Schumann designated several movements in these delightful piano pieces are transferred to the characters. Nijinsky is the Harlequin; Karsavina, Colombine, etc., while such pieces as *Dancing Letters* and *Paganini* are used as divertissements. The scene, with the two Victorian sofas at the back and Pierrot lying over the footlights, is charming. The principal characters are those of the *Commedia dell' Arte*, while the other dancers are dressed after the period of about 1830.

Le Dieu Bleu I have not seen but I transfer the following account of it from the "London Times" of February 28, 1913, in which the critic says that "it introduces us to Mme. Karsavina and M. Nijinsky in two new rôles which suit them well, and it gives good opportunities for the combination of music, dancing, and spectacle for which M. de Diaghilew's troup is famous — a combination designed this time to suggest what Goldsmith's Citizen of the World has in mind when he spoke of the 'furniture, frippery, and fireworks of China.' The scene is not precisely China in this case, but 'India of the fables,' which in the theatre comes to much the same thing, the point only being that it is the Far Orient, where a glamour of riotous colour is thrown over man's actions, and where gods and monsters are as near to us and as alive as the priests and populace who worship them.

"When the curtain goes up we see M. Bakst's design of a temple cut into a rock, with a glimpse of the sky seen through a cleft at the back, and in the middle a pool on which is floating (or ought to have been, for it was invisible last night) the sacred lotus. A young man is about to be initiated into the priesthood. He is surrounded by a crowd of worshippers, who bring offerings of fruits, flowers and peacocks to the shrine, and, generally speaking, occupy themselves in providing the requisite amount of furniture and frippery. Suddenly there is a tumult at the back, and a young girl (Mme. Karsavina) pushes her way in past the guards and falls at the feet of her lover, the would-be initiate, imploring him not to desert her for the priesthood.

He is at first indifferent, but gradually his religious ecstasy passes off as she recalls their old life together, and eventually, with an abrupt gesture, he throws himself into her arms. The priests, in consternation, hurry him off into the back premises, and after handcuffing the girl, leave her in the darkness, where (like Tamino in the caverns) she is told she will meet her trial and punishment. After long moments of suspense, during which night falls, she pushes open a door through which she sees a chance of escape, and immediately seven obscene monsters crawl out and are about to drag her with them when, in despair, she appeals to the sacred lotus in the pool. The lotus thereupon turns into the goddess, who rises with the blue god from the water. And then the fireworks began, for the blue god was M. Nijinsky, who at once set to work to draw the teeth, so to speak, of the monsters and to make even the trees and flowers 'bow themselves when he did dance,' thus proving satisfactorily that M. Salomon Reinach and his friends knew what they were about in maintaining that Orpheus came over the mountains from the East. The miracle accomplished, the priests come in to take note of it, the young lovers fall into each other's arms, the goddess retires to the lake, and the god goes up a staircase, which is disclosed behind by the removal of a mountain, the remains glued to it, in spite of the stage directions that he is supposed to fly to heaven. Being a god, he presumably thought he could please himself.

"The scenario does not give quite so many opportunities to M. Reynaldo Hahn as to MM. Bakst and Fokine, who are responsible for the pictorial and choreographic sides of the ballet. The theme associated with the god is the most striking. The dance with the peacocks is attractive, there are some beautiful moments when the young girl appeals to her lover, and their duet of joy at the end is spirited, but much of the music is lacking in character and the energy of the dance. It is written with the beautifully clear technique to which M. Hahn has accustomed us, but there is little driving force in it, and not a touch of passion in the scenes where passion is wanted to give contrast to the personal movements of the crowd or the calm atmosphere of the divinities."

Le Pavilion d'Armide is a graceful combination of two picturesque periods of romantic art, for a French Vicomte, storm-stayed on his travels, is offered hospitality by a Marquis, who lodges him in a pavilion of his castle, where the Gobelin tapestry comes to life during the night. The whole thing is, of course, a dream, in which the Vicomte sees in the Magician of the tapestry the person of his host, and himself plays the part of Rinaldo (the characters are those of Quinault's play set to music by Lulli and Gluck). When the change comes and Armida and her court come to life, what really comes to life is the court of Versailles; here is the Grand Monarque himself, and there the most enchanting group of knights in pink with feather head-dresses dance with ladies whose costumes combine the grace of Watteau with the conventional dancing-skirt with the happiest results.

In the dances from *Prince Igor*, accompanied by a chorus, the Russians loosen their restraint to a degree which would mean a totally unrestrained performance in the hands of another group of dancers. It is almost impossible to believe, after witnessing these wild Polovtsian dances, that the action has been perfectly ordered by Fokine and can be repeated exactly at any time. The ballet occupies almost all of the fourth act of Borodine's opera. I believe that the choruses to which these dances are performed were sung at a concert of the MacDowell Chorus in Carnegie Hall, March 3, 1911. The New York Winter Garden once utilized the music for a ballet. The scene used by the Russians, painted by Roerich, is marvelously suggestive of barbarism; the now languorous, now passionate music, pulsing with rhythm, is admirably adapted to dancing. Usually Mme. Fokina and Bolm are seen in these dances, but it is the ballet corps itself which becomes the important feature in their success.

"How excellently," says one foreign critic, "every means

that the theatre offers has been made use of to produce the desired effect; the menace of the coming cloud of barbarians that is to lie for centuries on the desolate face of Russia (for we are in the camp of the Polovtsians, forerunners of the great invasion); not the loud blustering of a Tamburlaine the Great, but the awful, quiet vigor, half melancholy, half playful, of a tribe that is but a little unit in the swarm; the infinite horizons of the steppe, with the line of the buried *tumuli* stretching away to endless times and places, down the centuries into Siberia, the long-drawn, resigned, egoless music (Borodine drew his themes from real Tartar-Mongol sources); the women that crouch, unconscious of themselves, or rise and stretch lazy limbs, and in the end fling themselves carelessly prone when their dance is over; the savage-joyful panther leaping of the men; the stamping feet and quick, nerve-racking beat of the drum; and more threatening than all, the gambolling of the boys , like kittens unwittingly preparing themselves for the future chase."

But whose is the guiding hand, the hand that combines the rhythms, the colors, and the human element in these works? It is Fokine's; without Fokine I do not see very well how these ballets could come into existence. (I am now speaking of Fokine, of course, entirely as a producer. He is also known as a dancer. One must bear in mind, also, that Nijinsky's three ballets — he contrived the action for *l'Après-midi d'un Faune, Jeux,* and *The Sacrifice to the Spring* — were very original and effective.) Until Fokine began to work, the ballet-master had been content to arrange all his *coryphées* in straight lines across the stage, each dancer making the same simultaneous movement as her neighbor. Fokine divined the ineffectiveness of this false symmetry. He divided his forces into many groups, each group a unit of movement. (The ultimate result of the application of this principle was Nijinsky's staging of *The Sacrifice to the Spring,* in which each dancer was set a separate simultaneous task.) Nor did Fokine allow any one group of dancers the whole of any movement in the music. He subdivided the movements into phrases. He really divided his ballet into choirs, just as Richard Strauss and Reger subdivided the orchestra, in which, in the time of Bellini and Donizetti, large bodies of the strings used to play in unison. Then each choir was given certain phrases to interpret, some in the background, some in the foreground, until the polyphony of the music was perfectly synchronized with the action of the ballet. Many of the ideas for Fokine's ballets were derived from pictures. It is possible to see at once the pictorial resemblance between *The Legend of Joseph* and Veronese's *The Marriage of Cana*, or between *Midas* and Mantegna's *Parnasse* in the Louvre. But Fokine also learned how to control movement, and how to preserve balance from pictures. In the Accademia di Belle Arti in Venice there is a room devoted to large paintings by Gentile Bellini and Vittore Carpaccio, depicting events in Venetian history. In one of them is a procession, and a study of the different groups of marchers and bystanders will give you an excellent idea of the effective and pictorial intricacy of a Fokine ballet. In *The Legend of Joseph* Fokine attains one of his most thrilling effects in the last scene, where the handmaidens of the refused Potiphar's wife, clad in black gauze, with bare arms and legs, wave their arms in a frenzy of hysterical disdain at the offending Joseph. Shortly after seeing the ballet, in walking through the Egyptian rooms of the British Museum, I came across an Egyptian fresco which almost seemed to me at first, in the exact spirit in which Fokine had caught its feeling, to be a photograph of the action I had seen on the stage.

Russians are natural dancers. It is said that only Russians and Poles can learn to do the mazurka properly, in which the women engage in that particular gliding step which someone characterized as the definite expression of Meredith's phrase, "gliding women." So, under the guidance of Fokine, with the inspiration which such music and color as are provided for them can give, the Russians engaged in the carrying out of these ballets easily rise to an unattainable (for other dancers) height of seeming spontaneity. They have that "like-to-do-it" and creative (as opposed to reproductive) air which every stage director knows is almost impossible to instill into a large company with any hope that it will be retained after the first performance. But the Russians never lose it. A ballet, given so often as *Sheherazade*, during a period extending over many seasons, always seems freshly produced. There are no slovenly details. The wild orgy of the Polovtsian dances of *Prince Igor* is invariably exposed with a feeling on the part of the spectator that he is witnessing the intense enjoyment of the participants.

Another important point is the variety in the ballets, a variety which covers not only subject and music, but also treatment in decoration and staging, so that such an ultra-modern work as *The Sacrifice to the Spring*, staged by Nijinsky in an attempt to emulate the style of the futurists in painting, with music by Strawinsky, who might be called a master of dissonance, and with decorations in hard and primitive colors by Roerich, finds itself naturally side by side with the charming and poetic *Sylphides,* gracefully staged by Fokine, with music by Chopin (orchestrated), and with decorations in pale green and white by Bakst. Of course, some ballets, because of their fables, or the nature of their music, naturally resemble one another. *Sheherazade*, *Cléopâtre*, *Thamar* all have certain points in common; so have *Les Sylphides, Carnaval* and *Papillons.* There is a resemblance between *Daphnis et Chloë, Narcisse,* and *l'Après-midi d'un Faune.* But it is easy to vary these likenesses by not putting them into juxtaposition by mingling them with the bizarre *Petrouchka,* the barbaric Polovtsian dances from *Prince Igor,* the idealistic *Spectre de la Rose,* with Weber's *Invitation to the Dance* as its accompaniment, the gorgeous and pompous *Legend of Joseph,* the frivolous *Midas,* the exotic *Le Dieu Bleu,* or the pageantry of the dances from Rimsky-Korsakow's *Sadko.*

It is impossible, of course, to ignore the genius and virtuosity of individual interpretation entirely in a study of the Russian Ballet, minimize as one may its importance. There have been very many pages written in an attempt to capture the charm and genius of Nijinsky on paper.[4] He has been described variously as "half-human, half-god," as a tongue of flame, and as a jet of water spurting from a fountain. The word "youth" expresses something of the wonder of this marvelous boy. He never seems to be doing anything difficult, and yet his command of technique is incredible. He always seems spontaneous, and yet I have been told that, like Olive Fremstad, he does not make the slightest movement of a finger which has not been carefully thought out. He seems to me to be the greatest of stage artists (and I include all concert musicians as well as opera singers and actors in this sweeping statement). I mean by this that he communicates more of beauty and emotion to me as a spectator than other interpretative artists do. All impressions of this sort are necessarily personal, but they do not for that reason lack value. It is essential, however, to see Nijinsky in a variety of parts to get his true measure. As the lover of the sylphs in *Les Sylphides* he is a pale *efféminé*, a Chopiniac, a charming Aubrey Beardsley drawing, a lovely thing in line, and grace, and sentiment. In *Petrouchka* he is a puppet, and — remarkable touch — a puppet with a soul. His performance in this ballet (the characters are marionettes, but the story is something like that of *Pagliacci*) is, perhaps, his most wonderful achievement. He suggests only the puppet in action; his facial expression never changes; yet the pathos is greater, more keenly carried over the footlights, than one would imagine possible under any conditions. I have seen Fokine in the same rôle, and although he gives you all the gestures, the result is not the same. It is genius that Nijinsky puts into his interpretation of the part. Who can ever forget Nijinsky as Petrouchka when thrown by his master into his queer black box, mad with love for the dancer, who, in turn, prefers the Moor puppet, rushing about waving his pathetically stiff arms in the air, and finally beating his way with his clenched fists through the paper window and cursing the stars? It is a more poignant expression of grief than most Romeos can give us. *Jeux* shows us the love games of a trio (two women and a man) searching for a tennis ball in a garden at twilight. It recalls itself to me chiefly for the *glissando* (the music is by Debussy) with which the ballet begins as the tennis ball bounces across the stage, followed by Nijinsky, who bounds across the broad stage of the Théâtre des Champs Elysées in Paris in two leaps. These leaps are triumphs of dexterity, grace of motion, and thrill, and he does not waste them. They have given rise to the rumor that Nijinsky's element is the air. In *l'Après-midi d'un Faune* he makes only one of these quick movements, but with such astonishing effect that on one occasion (it was the third time I had seen this stage arrangement of Debussy's prelude to Mallarmé's poem) my companion, a well-known dramatic critic who sits stolidly through performances by all the great tragedians, burst into tears. In *Sheherazade*, as the black slave of the harem who dominates the story of the ballet, Nijinsky utilizes his leap to dominate the bacchanale, which is the climax of that piece of sensual excitement. As the crowd of women, wives of the sultan, and black slaves, drunk with wine and lust, enter into the wildest dance, the negro in silver trousers in the centre of the stage leaps higher and higher straight into the air above the heads of his companions. . . The descent, with the indescribable curve of the legs, is something to be seen. In *Carnaval,* Nijinsky enacts the Harlequin with great roguishness and impertinence. To the piece called *Reconaissance* he dances with Karsavina, as Colombine, the most entrancing of polkas. His dancing of the piece called *Paganini,* however, is most memorable. At that point where the dominant seventh on E flat emerges through a deft use of the pedal, he represents the effect to perfection by suddenly sitting down, as a writer on the "London Times" once noted. It is not, as a matter of fact, as a mere dancer that Nijinsky excels, although he *does* excel even there, but it is in the poetic interpretation of his rôle, the genius in his playing, that he expresses so much more than his nearest rival. He is incomparable as a dancer, as you may very well see in works like *Carnaval* and *Les Sylphides,* in which dancing dominates the action; but even in these ballets he never loses sight of characterization, and the shaded values of ensemble.

Tamara Karsavina is a very beautiful woman, although her beauty has not the subtle quality of the more gifted Anna Pavlowa. She is an artist and a fine dancer, a mime of great talent. She fits more perfectly into an ensemble scheme than Pavlowa, who was once a member of this organization herself. She is delicate and flower-like and she suggests vice with a great degree of verisimilitude. Her Salome, with the painted roses on her nude knees and breasts, is a fragile bit of decadence. As the temptress Queen of *The Golden Cock* she suggests the strange perverted power of a Kundry, an Astarte, or a Loreley. In *The Legend of Joseph* it is her duty to sit at a table without changing her expression throughout almost an entire act. It is a difficult task; one must perceive the depths of the woman's boredom, which does not express itself even in impatience, and she must dominate the scene. She accomplishes her tasks beautifully, as she does also the long walk across the stage in stilted Venetian shoes at the close of the scene. In *Petrouchka* she is a fitting companion to Nijinsky, and her little dance with the cornet is a delicious and entrancing moment; her Chloë is exquisite, soft, Greek, and girlish, and in Ravel's ballet and in Florent Schmitt's *Salome* she dances *on her toes* in bare feet (remember that half the so-called "toe-dancers" resort to padded and reinforced slippers for their power). I never lack enthusiasm for Karsavina; but I cannot place her near Nijinsky.

The crescendo of eulogy with which these notes progress seems unavoidable. If one is in sympathy with the aims of this group of artists[5] (Gordon Craig is not, I believe), one must recognize the success with which they have carried them out. Naturally, there are flaws. Doboujinsky's costumes for *Midas* are certainly very hard in color; Stein-

berg's music for the same ballet, a series of futile brass blares; the story itself (Bakst *should* confine himself to painting), a bore. Massine is scarcely the dancer one would have chosen for so important a rôle as Joseph, which, on the other hand, he is suited to physically. Karsavina's portrayal of the ultimate emotions of Potiphar's wife is a little unconvincing. I do not even admire Bakst's setting for his very lovely costumes in *l'Après-midi d'un Faune*. But these are very small insects in the amber of enjoyment.
(*November, 1915*)

—From *Music After the Great War.* Schirmer, 1915

1. See chapter on Strawinsky./*Editor*
2. (Translation) "This is not the *l'Après-midi d'un Faune* of Stéphene Mallarmé; it is the musical prelude to that episode of panic, a short scene which precedes it:
   "A faun is sleeping;
   "Some nymphs deceive him;
   "A forgotten scarf satisfies his dream.
   "The curtain is lowered so that the poem begins with all his memories."
3. (Translation) "Accused of having 'offended morality,' Nijinsky hastened to satisfy M. Paul Souday by omitting his 'indecent mimicry' at the end of the ballet. However, his illusive possession of the fleeing nymph, that body lying on the veil still perfumed by her, that was beautiful!"
4. See chapter on Nijinsky./*Editor*
5. A very recent book has been published called *Diaghilev and the Ballets Russes* by Boris Kochno, Harpers, 1970. Mr. Kochno was Diaghilev's secretary and historian for the Company. Many of the dancers, choreographers, artists discussed in Van Vechten's text appear here in the years since Van Vechten wrote of them./*Editor*

Waslav Nijinsky

Serge de Diaghilew brought the dregs of the Russian Ballet to New York and, after a first greedy gulp, inspired by curiosity to get a taste of this highly advertised beverage, the public drank none too greedily. The scenery and the costumes, designed by Bakst, Roerich, Benois, and Larionow, and the music by Rimsky-Korsakow, Tcherepnine, Schumann, Borodine, Balakirew, and Strawinsky — especially Strawinsky — arrived. It was to be deplored, however, that Bakst had seen fit to replace the original décor of *Scheherazade* by a new setting in rawer colors, in which the flaming orange fairly burned into the ultramarine and green (readers of *A Rebours* will remember that des Esseintes designed a room something like this). A few of the dancers came, but of the best not a single one. Nor was Fokine, the dancer-producer, who devised the choreography for *The Firebird, Cléopâtre,* and *Petrouchka,* among the number, although his presence had been announced and expected. To those enthusiasts, and they included practically every one who had seen the Ballet in its greater glory, who had prepared their friends for an overwhelmingly brilliant spectacle, over-using the phrase, "a perfect union of the arts," the early performances in January, 1916, at the Century Theatre were a great disappointment. Often had we urged that the individual played but a small part in this new and gorgeous entertainment, but now we were forced to admit that the ultimate glamour was lacking in the ensemble, which was obviously no longer the glad, gay entity it once had been.

The picture was still there, the music (not always too well played) but the interpretation was mediocre. The agile Massine[1] could scarcely be called either a great dancer or a great mime. He had been chosen by Diaghilew for the rôle of Joseph in Richard Strauss's version of the Potiphar legend but, during the course of a London season carried through without the co-operation of Nijinsky, this was the only part allotted to him. In New York he interpreted, not without humor and with some technical skill, the incidental divertissement from Rimsky-Korsakow's opera, *The Snow-Maiden*, against a vivid background by Larionow. The uninspired choreography of this ballet was also ascribed to Massine by the programme, although probably in no comminatory spirit. In the small rôle of Eusebius in *Carnaval* and in the negligible part of the Prince in *The Firebird* he was entirely satisfactory, but it was impertinent of the Direction to assume that he would prove an adequate substitute for Nijinsky in rôles to which that dancer had formerly applied his extremely finished art.

Adolph Bolm contributed his portraits of the Moor in *Petrouchka*, of Pierrot in *Carnaval*, and of the Chief Warrior in the dances from *Prince Igor*. These three rôles completely express the possibilities of Bolm as a dancer or an actor, and sharply define his limitations. His other parts, Dakon in *Daphnis et Chloë*, Sadko, the Prince in *Thamar*, Amoun in *Cléopâtre*, the Slave in *Sheherazade*, and Pierrot in *Papillons*, are only variations on the three aforementioned themes. His friends often confuse his vitality and abundant energy with a sense of characterization and a skill as a dancer which he does not possess. For the most part he is content to express himself by stamping his heels and gnashing his teeth, and when, as in *Cléopâtre*, he attempts to convey a more subtle meaning to his general gesture, he is not very successful. Bolm is an interesting and useful member of the organization, but he could not make or unmake a season; nor could Gavrilow, who is really a fine dancer in his limited way, although he is unfortunately lacking in magnetism or any power of characterization.

But it was on the distaff side of the cast that the Ballet seemed pitifully undistinguished, even to those who did not remember the early Paris seasons when the roster included the names of Anna Pavlowa, Tamara Karsavina, Katerina Geltzer, and Ida Rubinstein. The leading feminine dancer of the troupe when it gave its first exhibitions in New York was Xenia Maclezova, who had not, so far as my memory serves, danced in any London or Paris season of the Ballet (except for one gala performance at the Paris Opéra which preceded the American tour) unless in some very menial capacity. This dancer, like so many others, had the technique of her art at her toes' ends. Sarah Bernhardt once told a reporter that the acquirement of technique never did any harm to an artist, and if one were not an artist it was not a bad thing to have. I have forgotten how many times Mlle. Maclezova could *pirouette* without touching the toe in the air to the floor, but it was some prodigious number. She was past mistress of the *entrechat* and other mysteries of the ballet academy. Here, however, her knowledge of her art seemed to end, in the subjugation of its very mechanism. She was very nearly lacking in those qualities of grace, poetry, and imagination with which great artists are freely endowed, and although she could not actually have been a woman of more than average weight, she often conveyed to the spectator an impression of heaviness. In such a work as *The Firebird* she really offended the eye. Far from interpreting the ballet, she gave you an idea of how it should not be done.

Her season with the Russians was terminated in very short order, and Lydia Lopoukova, who happened to be in America, and who, indeed, had already been engaged for certain rôles, was rushed into her vacant slippers. Now Mme. Lopoukova had charm as a dancer, whatever her deficiencies in technique. In certain parts, notably as Colombine in *Carnaval*, she assumed a roguish demeanor which was very fetching. As La Ballerine in *Petrouchka*, too, she met all the requirements of the action. But in *Le Spectre de la Rose, Les Sylphides, The Firebird,* and *La Princesse Enchantée,* (This was the name given that season to the Bluebird Variation from *The Sleeping Beauty./Editor*) she floundered hopelessly out of her element.

Tchernicheva, one of the lesser but more steadfast luminaries of the Ballet, in the rôles for which she was cast, the principal Nymph in *L'Après-midi d'un Faune,* Echo in *Narcisse,* and the Princess in *The Firebird,* more than fulfilled her obligations to the ensemble, but her opportunities in these mimic plays were not of sufficient importance to enable her to carry the brunt of the performances on her lovely shoulders. Flore Revalles was drafted, I understand, from a French opera company. I have been told that she sings — Tosca is one of her rôles — as well as she dances. That may very well be. To impressionable spectators she seemed a real femme fatale. Her Cléopâtre suggested to me a Parisian cocotte much more than an Egyptian queen. It would be blasphemy to compare her with Ida Rubinstein in this rôle — Ida Rubinstein, who was true Aubrey Beardsley! In Thamar and Zobeide, both to a great extent dancing rôles, Mlle. Revalles, both as dancer and actress, was but a frail substitute for Karsavina.

The remainder of the company was adequate, but not large, and the ensemble was by no means as brilliant as those who had seen the Ballet in London or Paris might have expected. Nor in the absence of Fokine, that master of detail, were performances sufficiently rehearsed. There was, of course, explanation in plenty for this disintegration. Gradually, indeed, the Ballet as it had existed in Europe had suffered a change. Only a miracle and a fortune combined would have sufficed to hold the original company intact. It was not held intact, and the war made further inroads on its integrity. Then, for the trip to America many of the dancers probably were inclined to demand double pay. Undoubtedly, Serge de Diaghilew had many more troubles than those which were celebrated in the public prints, and it must be admitted that, even with his weaker company, he gave us finer exhibitions of stage art than had previously been even the exception here.

In the circumstances, however, certain pieces, which were originally produced when the company was in the flush of its first glory, should never have been presented here at all. It was not the part of reason, for example, to pitchfork on the Century stage an indifferent performance of *Le Pavillon d'Armide*, in which Nijinsky once disported himself as the favorite slave, and which, as a matter of fact, requires a company of virtuosi to make it a passable diversion. *Cléopâtre*, in its original form, with Nijinsky, Fokine, Pavlowa, Ida Rubinstein, and others, hit all who saw it square between the eyes. The absurdly expurgated edition, with its inadequate cast, offered to New York, was but the palest shadow of the sensuous entertainment that had aroused all Paris, from the Batignolles to the Bastille. The music, the setting, the costumes — what else was left to celebrate? The altered choreography, the deplorable interpretation, drew tears of rage from at least one pair of eyes. It was quite incomprehensible also why *The Firebird*, which depended on the grace and poetical imagination of the filmiest and most fairy-like actress-dancer, should have found a place in the répertoire. It is the dancing equivalent of a coloratura soprano rôle in opera. Thankful, however, for the great joy of having reheard Strawinsky's wonderful score, I am willing to overlook this tactical error.

All things considered, it is small wonder that a large slice of the paying population of New York tired of the Ballet in short order. One reason for this cessation of interest was the constant repetition of ballets. In London and Paris the seasons as a rule have been shorter, and on certain evenings of the week opera has taken the place of the dance. It has been rare indeed that a single work has been repeated more than three or four times during an engagement. I have not found it stupid to listen to and look at perhaps fifteen performances of varying degrees of merit of *Petrouchka, Scheherazade, Carnaval*, and the dances from *Prince Igor*; I would rather see the Russian Ballet repeatedly, even as it existed in America, than four thousand five hundred and six Broadway plays or seventy-three operas at the Metropolitan once, but I dare say I may look upon myself as an exception.

At any rate, when the company entered upon a four weeks' engagement at the Metropolitan Opera House, included in the regular subscription season of opera, the subscribers groaned; many of them groaned aloud, and wrote letters to the management and to the newpapers. To be sure, during the tour which had followed the engagement at the Century the répertoire had been increased, but the company remained the same — until the coming of Waslav Nijinsky.

When America was first notified of the impending visit of the Russian Ballet it was also promised that Waslav Nijinsky and Tamara Karsavina would head the organization. It was no fault of the American direction or of Serge de Diaghilew that they did not do so. Various excuses were advanced for the failure of Karsavina to forsake her family in Russia and to undertake the journey to the United States but, whatever the cause, there seems to remain no doubt that she refused to come. As for Nijinsky, he, with his wife, had been a prisoner in an Austrian detention camp since the beginning of the war. Wheels were set grinding but wheels grind slowly in an epoch of international bloodshed, and it was not until March, 1916, that the Austrian ambassador at Washington was able to announce that Nijinsky had been set free.

I do not believe the coming to this country of any other celebrated person had been more widely advertised, although P.T. Barnum may have gone further in describing the charitable and vocal qualities of Jenny Lind. Nijinsky had been extravagantly praised, not only by the official press representatives but also by eminent critics and private persons, in adjectives which seemed to preclude any possibility of his living up to them. I myself had been among the paean singers. I had thrust "half-man, half-god" into print. "A flame!" cried some one. Another, "A jet of water from a fountain!" Such men in the street as had taken the trouble to consider the subject at all very likely expected the arrival of some stupendous and immortal monstrosity, a gravity-defying being with sixteen feet (at least), who bounded like a rubber ball, never touching the solid stage except at the beginning and end of the evening's performance.

Nijinsky arrived in April (1916). Almost immediately he gave vent to one of those expressions of temperament often associated with interpretative genius, the kind of thing I have described at some length in "Music And Bad Manners." He was not all pleased with the Ballet as he found it. Interviewed, he expressed his displeasure in the newspapers. The managers of the organization wisely remained silent, and a controversy was avoided, but the public had received a suggestion of petulance which could not contribute to the popularity of the new dancer.

Nijinsky danced for the first time in New York on the afternoon of April 12, at the Metropolitan Opera House. The pieces in which he appeared on that day were *Le Spectre de la Rose* and *Petrouchka*. Some of us feared that eighteen months in a detention camp would have stamped their mark on the dancer. As a matter of fact his connection with the Russian Ballet had been severed in 1913, a year before the war began. I can say for myself that I was probably a good deal more nervous than Nijinsky on the occasion of his first appearance in America. It would have been a cruel disappointment to me to discover that his art had deteriorated during the intervening years since I had last seen him. My fears were soon dissipated. A few seconds after he, as the Rose Ghost, had bounded through the window, it was evident that he was in possession of all his powers; nay, more, that he had added to the refinement and polish of his style. I had called Nijinsky's dancing perfection in years gone by, because it so far surpassed that of his nearest rival; now he had surpassed himself. True artists, indeed, have a habit of accomplishing this feat. I may call to your attention the careers of Olive Fremstad, Yvette Guilbert, and Marie Tempest. Later I learned that this first impression might be relied on. Nijinsky, in sooth, has now no rivals upon the stage. One can only compare him with himself.

The Weber-Gautier dance-poem, from the very beginning until the end, when he leaps out of the girl's chamber into the night, affords this great actor-dancer one of his most grateful opportunities. It is in this very part, perhaps, which requires almost unceasing exertion for nearly twelve minutes, that Nijinsky's powers of co-ordination, mental, imaginative, muscular, are best displayed. His dancing is accomplished in that flowing line, without a break between poses and gestures, which is the despair of all novices and almost all other virtuosi. After a particularly difficult leap or toss of the legs or arms, it is a marvel to observe how, without an instant's pause to regain his poise, he rhythmically glides into the succeeding gesture. His dancing has the unbroken quality of music, the balance of great painting, the meaning of fine literature, and the emotion inherent in all these arts. There is something of transmutation in his performances; he becomes an alembic, transforming movement into a finely wrought and beautiful work of art. The dancing of Nijinsky is first an imaginative triumph, and the spectator, perhaps, should not be interested in further dissection of it, but a more intimate observer must realize that behind this the effect produced depends on his supreme command of his muscles. It is not alone the final informing and magnetized imaginative quality that most other dancers lack; it is also just this muscular co-ordination. Observe Gavrilow in the piece under discussion, in which he gives a good imitation of Nijinsky's general style, and you will see that he is unable to maintain this rhythmic continuity.

Nijinsky's achievements become all the more remarkable when one remembers that he is working with an imperfect physical medium. Away from the scene he is an insignificant figure, short and ineffective in appearance. Aside from the pert expression of his eyes, he is like a dozen other young Russians. Put him unintroduced into a drawing-room with Jacques Copeau, Orchidée, Doris Keane, Bill Haywood, the Baroness de Meyer, Paulet Thévenaz, the Marchesa Casati, Marcel Duchamp, Cathleen Nesbitt, H.G. Wells, Anna Pavlowa, Rudyard Chennevière, Vladimir Rebikow, Henrie Waste, and Isadora Duncan, and he probably would pass entirely unnoticed. On the stage it may be observed that the muscles of his legs are over-developed and his ankles are too large; that is, if you are in the mood for picking flaws, which most of us are not in the presence of Nijinsky in action. Here, however, stricture halts confounded; his head is set on his shoulders in a manner to give satisfaction to a great sculptor, and his torso, with its slender waist line, is quite beautiful. On the stage, Nijinsky makes of himself what he will. He can look tall or short, magnificent or ugly, fascinating or repulsive. Like all great interpretative artists, he remoulds himself for his public appearances. It is under the electric light in front of the painted canvas that he becomes a personality, and that personality is governed only by the scenario of the ballet he is representing.

From the day of Nijinsky's arrival, the ensemble of the Ballet improved; somewhat of the spontaneity of the European performances was regained; a good deal of the glamour was recaptured; the loose lines were gathered taut, and the choreography of Fokine (Nijinsky is a director as well as a dancer) was restored to some of its former power. He has appeared in nine rôles in New York during the two short seasons in which he has been seen with the Russian Ballet here; the Slave in *Scheherazade,* Petrouchka, the Rose Ghost, the Faun, the Harlequin in *Carnaval,* Narcisse, Till Eulenspiegel, and the principal male rôles of *La Princesse Enchantée* and *Les Sylphides.* To enjoy the art of Nijinsky completely, to fully appreciate his genius, it is necessary not only to see him in a variety of parts, but also to see him in the same rôle many times.

Study the detail of his performance in *Scheherazade,* for example. Its precision alone is noteworthy. Indeed, precision is a quality we see exposed so seldom in the theatre that when we find it we are almost inclined to hail it as genius. The rôle of the Slave in this ballet is perhaps Nijinsky's scenic masterpiece — exotic eroticism expressed in so high a key that its very existence seems incredible on our puritanic stage, and yet with such great art (the artist always expresses himself with beauty) that the intention is softened by the execution. Before the arrival of this dancer, *Scheherazade* had become a police court scandal.[2] There had been talk of a "Jim Crow" performance in which the blacks were to be separated from the whites in the harem, and I am told that our provincial police magistrates even wanted to replace the "mattresses" — so were the divans of the sultanas described in court — by rocking chairs! But to the considerably more vivid *Scheherazade* of Nijinsky no exception was taken. This strange, curious, head-wagging, simian creature, scarce human, wriggled through the play, leaving a long streak of lust and terror in his wake. Never did Nijinsky as the Negro Slave touch the Sultana, but his subtle and sensuous fingers fluttered close to her flesh, clinging once or twice questioningly to a depending tassel. Pierced by the javelins of the Sultana's men, the Slave's death struggle might have been revolting and gruesome. Instead Nijinsky carried the eye rapidly upward with his tapering feet as they balanced for the briefest part of a second straight high in the air, only to fall inert with so brilliantly swift a movement that the aesthetic effect grappled successfully with the feeling of disgust which might have been aroused. This was acting, this was characterization, so completely merged in rhythm that the result became a perfect whole and not a combination of several intentions, as so often results from the work of an actor-dancer.

The heart-breaking Petrouchka, the roguish Harlequin, the Chopiniac of *Les Sylphides* — all were offered to our view; and *Narcisse*, in which Nijinsky not only did some very beautiful dancing, but posed (as the Greek youth admired himself in the mirror of the pool) with such utter and arresting grace that even here he awakened a new kind of emotion. In *La Princesse Enchantée* he merely danced, but how he danced! Do you who saw him still remember those flickering fingers and toes? "He winketh with his eyes, he speaketh with his feet, he teacheth with his fingers," is written in the Book of Proverbs, and the writer might have had in mind Nijinsky in *La Princesse Enchantée*. All these parts were differentiated, all completely realized, in the threefold intricacy of this baffling art, which perhaps is not an art at all until it is so realized, when its plastic, rhythmic, and histrionic elements become an entity.

After a summer in Spain and Switzerland with Nijinsky, the Russian Ballet returned to America for a second season, opening at the Manhattan Opera House October 16, 1916. It is always a delight to hear and see performances in this theatre, and it was found that the brilliance of the Ballet was much enhanced by its new frame.[3] The season, however, opened with a disappointment. It had been announced that Nijinsky would dance on the first night his choreographic version of Richard Strauss's tone-poem, *Till Eulenspiegel*. It is not the first time that a press agent has made a false prophecy. While rehearsing the new work Nijinsky twisted his ankle, and during the first week of the engagement he did not appear at all. This was doubly unfortunate, because the company was weaker than it had been the previous season, lacking both Massine and Tchernicheva. The only novelty (for America) produced during the first week was an arrangement of the divertissement from Rimsky-Korsakow's opera, *Sadko*, which had already been given a few times in Paris and London by the Ballet, never with conspicuous success. The second week of the season, Nijinsky returned to appear in three rôles, the Faun, Till Eulenspiegel, and the Slave in *Scheherazade*. Of his performance to Debussy's lovely music I have written elsewhere;[4] nor did this new vision cause me to revise my opinions.

Till Eulenspiegel is the only new ballet the Russians have produced in America. (*Soleil de Nuit* was prepared in Europe, and performed once at the Paris Opéra before it was seen in New York. Besides, it was an arrangement of dances from an opera which is frequently given in Russia and which has been presented at the Opéra-Comique in Paris.) The chef d'orchestre, Pierre Monteaux, refused to direct performances of this work, on the ground that the composer was not only a German, but a very much alive and active German patriot. On the occasions, therefore, that *Till* was performed in New York, the orchestra struggled along under the baton of Dr. Anselm Goetzl. In selecting this work and in his arrangement of the action Nijinsky was moved, no doubt, by consideration for the limitations of the company as it existed. The scenery and costumes by Robert E. Jones, of New York, were decidedly diverting — the best work this talented young man has done, I think. Over a deep, spreading background of ultramarine, the crazy turrets of mediaeval castles leaned dizzily to and fro. The costumes were exaggerations of the exaggerated fashions of the Middle Ages. Mr. Jones added feet of stature to the already elongated peaked headdresses of the period. The trains of the velvet robes, which might have extended three yards, were allowed to trail the full depth of the Manhattan Opera House stage. The colors were oranges, reds, greens, and blues, those indeed of Bakst's *Scheherazade,* but so differently disposed that they made an entirely dissimilar impression. The effect reminded one spectator of a Spanish omelet.

In arranging the scenario, Nijinsky followed in almost every detail Wilhelm Klatte's description of the meaning of the music, which is printed in programme books whenever the tone-poem is performed, without Strauss's authority, but sometimes with his sanction. Nijinsky was quite justified in altering the end of the work, which hangs the rogue-hero, into another practical joke. His version of this episode fits the music and, in the original Till Eulenspiegel stories, Till is not hanged, but dies in bed. The keynote of Nijinsky's interpretation was gaiety. He was as utterly picaresque as the work itself; he reincarnated the spirit of Gil Blas; indeed, a new quality crept into stage expression through this characterization. Margaret Wycherly, one of the most active admirers of the dancer, told me after the first performance that she felt that he had for the first time leaped into the hearts of the great American public, whose appreciation of his subtler art as expressed in *Narcisse, Petrouchka,* and even *Scheherazade,* had been more moderate. There were those who protested that this was not the Till of the German legends, but any actor who attempts to give form to a folk or historical character, or even a character derived from fiction, is forced to run counter to many an observer's preconceived ideas.

"It is an error to believe that pantomime is merely a way of doing without words," writes Arthur Symons, "that it is merely the equivalent of words. Pantomime is thinking overheard. It begins and ends before words have formed themselves, in a deeper consciousness than that of speech. And it addresses itself, by the artful limitations of its craft, to universal human experience, knowing that the moment it departs from those broad lines it will become unintelligible. It risks existence on its own perfection, as the rope-dancer does, to whom a false step means a downfall. And it appeals democratically to people of all nations. . . And pantomime has that mystery which is one of the requirements of true art. To watch it is like dreaming. How silently, in dreams, one gathers the unheard sounds of words from the lips that do not make pretense of saying them! And does not everyone know that terrifying impossibility of speaking which fastens one to the ground for the eternity of a second, in what is the new, perhaps truer, computation of time in dreams? Something like that sense of suspense seems to hang over the silent actors in pantomime, giving them a nervous exaltation, which has its subtle, immediate effect upon us, in tragic and comic situations. The silence becomes an atmosphere, and with a very curious power of giving distinction to form and motion. I do not see why people should ever break silence on the stage except to speak poetry. Here, in pantomime, you have a gracious, expressive silence, beauty of gesture, a perfectly discreet appeal to the emotions, a transposition of the world into an elegant accepted convention."

Arthur Symons wrote these words before he had seen the Russian Ballet, before the Russian Ballet, as we know it, existed, indeed, before Nijinsky had begun to dance in public, and he felt that the addition of poetry and music to pantomime — the Wagner music-drama in other words — brought about a perfect combination of the arts. Nevertheless, there is an obvious application of his remarks to the present instance. There is indeed, the quality of a dream about the characters Nijinsky presents to us. I remember once, at a performance of the Russian Ballet, I sat in a box next to a most intelligent man, a writer himself; I was meeting him for the first time, and he was seeing the Ballet for the first time. Before the curtain rose he had told me that dancing and pantomime were very pretty to look at, but that he found no stimulation in watching them, no mental and spiritual exaltation, such as might follow a performance of *Hamlet*. Having seen Nijinsky, I could not agree with him — and this indifferent observer became that evening himself a fervent disciple of the Ballet. For Nijinsky gave him, he found, just what his ideal performance of Shakespeare's play might have given him, a basis for dreams, for thinking, for poetry. The ennobling effect of all great and perfect art, after the primary emotion, seems to be to set our minds wandering in a thousand channels, to suggest new outlets. Pater's experience before the *Mona Lisa* is only unique in its intense and direct expression.

No writer, no musician, no painter, can feel deep emotion before a work of art without expressing it in some way, although the expression may be a thousand leagues removed from the inspiration. And how few of us can view the art of Nijinsky without emotion! To the painter he gives a new sense of proportion, to the musician a new sense of rhythm, while to the writer he must perforce immediately suggest new words; better still, new meanings for old words. Dance, pantomime, acting, harmony, all these divest themselves of their worn out accoutrements and appear, as if clothed by magic, in garments of unheard-of novelty; hue, texture, cut, and workmanship are all a surprise to us. We look enraptured, we go away enthralled, and perhaps even unconsciously a new quality creeps into our own work. It is the same glamour cast over us by contemplation of the Campo Santo at Pisa, or the Roman Theatre at Orange, or the Cathedral at Chartres — the inspiration for one of the most word-jewelled books in any language — or the New York skyline at twilight as one sails away into the harbor, or a great iron crane which lifts tons of alien matter in its gaping jaw. Great music can give us this feeling, the symphonies of Beethoven, Mozart's *Don Giovanni,* Schubert's C major symphony, or César Franck's D minor, *The Sacrifice to the Spring* of Strawinsky, *l'Après-midi d'un Faune* of Debussy, Chabrier's Rhapsody, *España;* great interpretative musicians can give it to us, Ysaye at his best, Paderewski, Marcella Sembrich in song recital; but how few artists on the stage suggest even as much as the often paltry lines of the author, the often banal music of the composer! There is an *au delà* to all great interpretative art, something that remains after story, words, picture, and gesture have faded vaguely into that storeroom in our memories where are concealed these lovely ghosts of ephemeral beauty, and the artist who is able to give us this is blessed even beyond his knowledge, for to him has been vouchsafed the sacred kiss of the gods. This quality cannot be acquired, it cannot even be described, but it can be felt. With its beneficent aid the interpreter not only contributes to our pleasure, he broadens our horizon, adds to our knowledge and capacity for feeling.[5]

As I read over these notes I realize that I have not been able to discover flaws in the art of this young man. It seems to me that in his chosen medium he approaches perfection. What he attempts to do, he always does perfectly. Can one say as much for any other interpreter? But it is a difficult matter to give the spirit of Nijinsky, to describe his art on paper, to capture the abundant grace, the measureless poetry, the infinite illusion of his captivating motion in ink. Who can hope to do it? Future generations must take our word for his greatness. We can do little more than call it that. I shall have served my purpose if I have succeeded in this humble article in bringing back to those who have seen him a flashing glimpse of the imaginative actuality.
(*January 16, 1917*)

—From *Interpreters and Interpretations,* Knopf, 1917

1. Massine: For a recent retrospective and illustrated profile on the

career of Massine, see *Dance Magazine,* November, 1969. / *Editor*
2. It is interesting to note that "censorship" in 1916 had heavy overtones of racism. In the Twenties a celebrated court case of another genre and gender involved a play written by and starring Mae West. / *Editor*
3. Manhattan Opera House: A history of the theatre and its resident company was published as *Oscar Hammerstein's Manhattan Opera Company,* University of Oklahoma Press, 1966. / *Editor*
4. A critical discussion of Nijinsky as the Faun in *l'Après-midi d'un Faune,* is included in the "Secret of the Russian Ballet" chapter. / *Editor*
5. In 1972 a new biography was published on Nijinsky that is a valuable addition for interested readers. It is *Nijinsky* by Richard Buckle, published by Simon & Schuster. / *Editor*

Anna Pavlowa and Mikail Mordkin, 1910

More than two-thirds of the boxes at the Metropolitan Opera House were still filled with their occupants at half after twelve last night. It was not a performance of *Götterdämmerung* without cuts that kept a fashionable Monday night audience in its seats, but the American début of Anna Pavlowa, the Russian dancer from the Imperial Opera in St. Petersburg. Mme. Pavlowa appeared in a revival of *Coppélia,* which was given at the Metropolitan for the first time since the season of 1904-5. As this was preceded by a performance of *Werther,* the ballet did not commence until after eleven, and it was nearly one before it was finished.

However, Mme. Pavlowa easily held most of her audience. It is safe to say that such dancing has not been seen on the local stage during the present generation. If Pavlowa were a regular member of the Metropolitan Opera Company it would also be safe to prophecy a revival of favor for the classic ballet.

The little dancer is lithe and exquisitely formed. When she first appeared just after the curtain rose there was a dead silence. She received no welcome. She wore the conventional ballet dress and her dark hair was bound back with a blue band.

After the first waltz, which immediately follows her entrance, the audience burst into vociferous applause, which was thereafter repeated at every possible opportunity. Pavlowa received an ovation of the sort which is seldom given to anybody at this theatre.

And her dancing deserved it. To begin with, her technique is of a sort to dazzle the eye. The most difficult tricks of the art of the dancer she executed with supreme ease. She even went further. There were gasps of astonishment and bursts of applause after several of her remarkable feats, all of which were accomplished with the greatest ease and lightness.

Grace, a certain sensuous charm, and a decided sense of humor are other qualities which she possesses. In fact, it would be difficult to conceive a dancer who so nearly realizes the ideal of this sort of dancing.

In the first act she was assisted at times by Mikail Mordkin, who also comes from St. Petersburg, and who is only second to Pavlowa as a remarkable dancer. Their *pas de deux* near the end of the act was perhaps the best-liked bit of the evening. It was in the second act in her impersonation of the doll that Pavlowa disclosed her charming sense of humor.

At this time it is impossible to write any more about this dancer, but there is no doubt that she will prove a great attraction while she remains in New York.

— *The New York Times,* March 1, 1910

The second appearance at the Metropolitan Opera House

of the two Russian dancers, Anna Pavlowa and Mikail Mordkin, was undoubtedly the feature of the performance which was given there last night for the benefit of the pension and endowment fund of that institution.[1] The auditorium was packed for the occasion, and the total receipts were somewhere in the neighborhood of $15,000.

Very late in the evening before these two dancers had appeared in Delibes's ballet *Coppélia*. Last night they appeared alone without the assistance of the somewhat ragged corps de ballet of the Metropolitan Opera House in two divertissements, which were so entirely different from anything they had done in *Coppélia* that anyone who had seen their previous performance would have had difficulty in recognizing them.

Such dancing has not been seen in New York in recent years, and last night's audience manifested its feeling as heartily as had that of Monday evening.

Early in the evening the curtains parted on a woodland scene which left a large open space on the stage. The orchestra played an adagio of Bleichmann's. First Mordkin darted on to the scene dressed as a savage. Pavlowa followed him. The two danced together and then alone. Mordkin whirled for long seconds on one foot, with the other foot pointed at right angles from his body. He did another dance, in which he shot arrows from a huge bow behind his shoulder. The celerity, the grace, the rhythm of his terpsichorean feats were indescribable in their effect.

Pavlowa twirled on her toes. With her left toe pointed out behind her, maintaining her body poised to form a straight line with it, she leapt backward step by step on her right foot. She swooped into the air like a bird and floated down. She never dropped. At times she seemed to defy the laws of gravitation. The divertissement ended with Pavlowa, supported by Mordkin, flying through the air, circling his body around and around. The curtain fell. The applause was deafening. Again and again the two were called before the footlights.

Later in the evening the two danced again to music from

a ballet of Glazunow's. This special divertissement was called *Autumn*. The music was gay and furious in its rhythm. The two in Greek draperies dashed about the stage, veiled in a background of floating gauze. The music became wilder and wilder, and wilder and wilder grew the pace of the two. The Bacchanalian finale, in which Pavlowa was finally swept to the earth, held the audience in tense silence for a moment after it was over, and then the applause broke out again. The curtain calls after this dance were innummerable.

— *The New York Times*, March 2, 1910

1. This review of Pavlova and Mordkin in their second appearance in New York is very bad Van Vechten writing. Its only excuse is the early date of composition (March, 1910). It is included in this collection because of its historical significance in recording the event. It shows, by comparison, how Van Vechten's critical writing on the dance improved in the later appearances — even those a few months later — especially, when he was inspired by the best of the Russian Ballet or a Nijinsky. / *Editor*

Mme. Pavlowa and Mr. Mordkin introduced two new dances to this public at The New Theatre yesterday afternoon. Both of the new dances were better suited to the smaller stage of that theatre than *Coppélia*. In the first Pavlowa danced alone to Saint-Saëns's *Le Cygne*, played on the solo violin with a harp accompaniment. This dancer's poetic conception of the swan was an achievement of the highest order of imagination. It is the most exquisite specimen of her art which she has yet given to this public.

Immediately after, to the accompaniment of Chopin's C sharp major waltz, played on the pianoforte, Mordkin and Pavlowa danced a *pas de deux* in early nineteenth century costumes. This was as beautiful in its way as the other dance. The two will be repeated tonight at The New Theatre.

— *The New York Times*, March 18, 1910

To say that history repeated itself yesterday afternoon at the Metropolitan Opera House, when Pavlowa and Mordkin reappeared with their own company, to give for the first time here a programme all by themselves, would be to express the case very mildly, indeed. It might almost be said that history was made on this occasion. It is doubtful if such dancing has been seen on the Metropolitan stage save when these two Russians were here last season, and it is certain that there never has been more enthusiasm let loose in the theatre on a Saturday afternoon than there was yesterday.

The programme included two complete ballets and several divertissements, and from 2:30 to 5:30, with intermissions now and then, Pavlowa and Mordkin gave exhibitions of their highly finished and poetic art.

The afternoon began with a performance of Adolphe Adam's ballet *Giselle,* which has never been given before on this stage and probably not often in New York, although it was seen here in 1842, one year after the original Paris production, which occurred at the Opéra, with Carlotta Grisi as the unhappy heroine.

The subject for the ballet was taken from Heinrich Heine's book about Germany. "There exists a tradition of nocturnal dancers, known in the Slavic countries as the Wilis. The Wilis are betrothed girls who have died before their marriage. These poor creatures cannot remain tranquil in their tombs. In their hearts, which have stopped beating, in their dead feet, exists a love for dancing which they have not been able to satisfy during their lives. At midnight they rise and gather in troops, and unfortunate is the young man who encounters them. He is forced to dance with them until he falls dead.

"Garbed in their bridal robes, with crowns of orange blossoms on their heads and brilliant rings on their fingers, the Wilis dance in the moonlight like elves, their faces, although white as snow, are beautifully young. They smile with a joy so perfidious, they call you with so much seduction, their manner gives so many soft promises that these dead bacchantes are irresistible."

Théophile Gautier is said to have run across this passage one day and to have exclaimed involuntarily: "What a subject for a ballet!"

Whereupon he sat down and wrote across the top of a blank sheet of paper: "Les Wilis, un ballet." However, he probably would have forgotten all about it if he had not encountered a composer at the Opéra that same evening. The result was that he and Saint-Georges collaborated on the book and Adam wrote the music. Coralli, the ballet master of the Opéra at that period, had enough to do with the book so that his name appears on the title page with the others.

This passage from Heine afterwards attracted the eyes of other composers and librettists. The English composer, Loder, used the idea for his most successful opera, *The Night Dancers,* produced shortly after *Giselle,* and Puccini wrote his first opera, *Le Villi,* on the same theme.

Carlotta Grisi danced the ballet and *Giselle* became the rage. Flowers, hats, gloves, dogs, and horses were named after her. The ballet was done almost immediately in England and America. But, strangely enough, it disappeared from the répertoire of the Opéra until it was revived in 1863 with Mlle. Mouravieva, herself a Russian from Moscow. She was described by one critic of the day as having plenty of technique but "not an atom of poetry."

In Russia *Giselle* has always been popular, and Mrs. Newmarch says that it was Tschaikowsky's ideal ballet when he composed his *Lac des Cygnes.* In Paris the past season has seen a revival of it, again by Russians.

The music is gently fragrant, a little faded here and there, but a pretty score, and one of Adam's best. Cuts were made freely. In fact, almost one-half of the music had been taken out, and this was probably for the best, as far as present-day audiences are concerned. There was one interpolation. In the first act a waltz from Glazunow's *Raymonda* was introduced, which was very much as if some conductor had performed *Also Sprach Zarathustra* somewhere in *Fra Diavolo.*

Mlle. Pavlowa yesterday revivified this honeyfied and sentimental score of Adam's, full of the sad, gray splendor of the time of Louis Philippe. Grisi is said to have been gently melancholy in it, but Pavlowa was probably more than that. Her poetic conception of the betrothed girl's madness when she finds that her lover has deceived her, and her death, came very close to being tragic. It is almost impossible to describe the poetry of her dancing in the second act, where as one of the Wilis she engages in the wildest sort of measures under the forest trees.

Mr. Mordkin had no dancing to do in this ballet, but in appearance and action he was superb. For some reason the programme referred to the Wilis as "fairies," which can scarcely be regarded as an accurate translation.

The second part of the programme consisted of divertissements beginning with a very pretty performance of Liszt's Second Rhapsodie by Mme. Pajitzkaia, and the corps de ballet. After this Pavlowa and Mordkin danced the adagio of Bleichmann and the Tschaikowsky Variation, in which they were often seen last year. After the bow and arrow dance, with which this divertissement concludes, it seemed as if Mr. Mordkin would never be able to leave the stage, the applause was so deafening and so long continued.

Some Russian dances followed to music from Glinka's *A Life for the Czar,* not by Tschaikowsky, as the programme stated, and this section of the programme was completed with the *Bacchanale* from Glazunow's ballet, *The Seasons,* in which Pavlowa and Mordkin swept the audience almost literally out of their chairs. This dance to many reaches the heights of choreographic art.

The ballet which concluded the programme was called *The Legend of Azyiade,* and was doubtless suggested by a performance of Rimsky-Korsakow's symphony *Scheherazade* as a ballet at the Paris Opéra last summer. However, Mordkin had arranged for this occasion an entirely different story and the music was taken from many sources although some of the themes from Rimsky-Korsakow's symphony were retained. Among the dances introduced was one from Bourgault-Ducoudray's opera *Tamara*, distinctly Persian in character, and quite extraordinarily sensuous in its rhythm and tonal monotony. Several other composers, including Chaminade and Glazunow, were called upon to contribute.

Pavlowa as the captive princess was as bewitching as possible, and Mordkin was so beautifully kinglike that many in the audience were heard to condemn the escape of the captive princess at the close as an unhappy ending.

The small group of dancers which accompanies Pavlowa and Mordkin on this tour are most of them Russians and seemed to indicate that in Russia as well as America Pavlowa and Mordkin are unsurpassed. The corps de ballet appeared to special advantage in *The Legend of Azyiade*.

To Mr. Mordkin the highest praise is due for his work as a ballet master, for it was he who arranged the steps for all the dances and the programme of the afternoon which contained just the correct amount of diversity.

Theodore Stier, the conductor of the Bechstein Hall concerts in London, made his first American appearance and gave an especially poetic reading of *Giselle*, and put the requisite amount of sensuousness in the music for the Arabian ballet. The orchestra's performance of the music to which Mr. Mordkin dances the bow and arrow dance would suggest that more rehearsals might do it benefit if it were not remembered that the Metropolitan Opera House orchestra last season never succeeded in playing it even respectably.

—*The New York Times,* October 16, 1910.

Anna Pavlowa, 1920

It may seem a little unprecise to describe a personality so

vivid as that of Anna Pavlowa as old-fashioned. Yet she is old-fashioned, in the delightful sense of that epithet; not old-fashioned like things of the day before yesterday, the slang of 1910, the bicycle, or "ballroom dancing," but like the lambrequins, wax-flowers, shell-baskets, glazed chintzes, and mezzotints of our grandmothers, which the Baron de Meyer has so pleasantly revived.

She is the last of the great school of classic dancers, a fragrant reminiscence of the early nineteenth century, born of the same tradition as Taglioni and Fanny Elssler and Carlotta Grisi, and as great as these, perhaps greater than these. With the modern movement in dancing, with which she mistakenly allied herself at one time in her career, she has nothing whatever to do. Save in such a divertissement as *Les Sylphides*, she was entirely out of place in the Russian Ballet, into which the more nearly contemporary art of Karsavina fitted so neatly. Even less appropriately can Pavlowa be identified with Isadora Duncan and the so-called revival of the dances of the Greeks. The Russian has, to be sure, assumed character rôles, but she is only supreme as the exponent of the classic ballet in works like *Coppélia*, in the true Italian tradition, or Adolphe Adam's *Giselle*. In Glazunow's *Bacchanale,* which she and Mordkin performed with so much abandon, she may have appeared to commit herself to the new freedom, but it was to be observed that even in this number she preserved the conventions of the classic school by wearing tights and ballet-slippers.

Her only rival in coeval choreographic history, Adeline Genée, a far inferior performer, was practically vanquished from the day that Pavlowa first set foot on the London stage, Genée, who had enjoyed her hour, was roguish, witty, twinkling, and saucy, (Saucy is a word that has almost fallen into disuse because no new girls are born to fit it. Perhaps Marie Tempest was the last. She *was* saucy. Another epithet, piquant, frequently applied to *sauces* for steaks, might with equal justice be applied to *her*.) but the Scandinavian not only lacked the finished technique of the

Russian, she also wanted her tragic grace. For the mask of Pavlowa is truly tragic, a face of haunting intensity and hurt loveliness. It may be that with her passing the school of toe-dancing will also pass, but it may also be remarked that nothing dies so long as any one is great enough to keep it alive.
(*October 7, 1920*)

— "Pastiches et Pistaches," *The Reviewer,* January, 1924: Richmond, Virginia.

Swan Lake Ballet

Tchaikowsky's four-act ballet, *Le Lac des Cygnes,*[1] received what was probably its first production in New York yesterday afternoon at the Metropolitan Opera House. The occasion also marked the return of the Russian Ballet and the first American appearance of Katerina Geltzer,[2] the first dancer of the Moscow Imperial Opera, who created the sort of an impression which is only conjured up by great dancers.

Le Lac des Cygnes is an early work of the Russian composer, written in 1876, when he was in a period of great mental and physical unrest. Its opus number is 20 and it is preceded in his list of works by nothing more important than the first and second symphonies, the first string quartet, and the orchestral fantasie, *The Tempest.*

Tchaikowsky, like other Russians, was a devotee of dancing, and Begichev, then stage director of the Opera at Moscow, proposed to him that he write a ballet. The composer agreed, but stipulated for a fantastic subject from the chivalric age. His favorite ballet at that period was *Giselle,* for which Théophile Gautier wrote the book and Adolphe Adam the music. Begichev himself sketched out the plot for *Le Lac des Cygnes.*

We are introduced in the first act to Siegfried, a Prince of the fifteenth century. He has just come of age, and the opening scene is a celebration of this event. As the festivities draw to a conclusion a flock of swans wings its way across the sky and Siegfried and his friends depart to shoot them.

When they near the swans, however, they perceive beautiful young maidens, who tell how they are in the power of a sorcerer and may only achieve their human form at night. Siegfried falls in love with the most beautiful of these swan maidens, and she tells him that she may escape the enchantment if she finds a man who will be true to his love for her. He promises to return to claim her.

The sorcerer, however, summons a spirit to impersonate Siegfried's swan love, Odetta, and Siegfried, deceived, proves false to his promise, and Odetta returns to the sorcerer's power. In despair, on learning the truth, he attacks the demon, who hurls him into the lake. He has now proved his love, and Odetta regains her original form, but now that Siegfried is dead, she, too, seeks death in the lake.

This romantic tale did not suffice for the purposes of the Moscow ballet master, and he asked Tchaikowsky to write a suite of national dances for the third act. They have nothing whatever to do with the story, but they serve their purpose as pretty character episodes.

The music is not by any means Tchaikowsky at his best. Both *La Belle au Bois Dormant* and *Casse-Noisette* are much better ballets. Some of the music of the first and second acts is banal, and there is a good deal of padding, mainly in the shape of long sequences, but every now and then, of course, there is charming music. The waltzes are especially pretty and the dramatic music is usually good enough for its purpose. A good deal of it was cut yesterday.

It is a curious fact the principal theme of the ballet, which recurs again and again, is practically the same as the "Mystery of the Name" theme from *Lohengrin,* the notes to which Lohengrin sings, "Nie sollst du mich befragen." Now, Tchaikowsky visited Bayreuth in 1876, the year he wrote the ballet. Of course, *Lohengrin* was not sung at Bayreuth before 1894, however.

In the ballet of *The Sleeping Beauty* there is another curious Wagner reminiscence. The theme representing the sleeping Princess has a close analogy with that depicting the sleep of Brünnhilde. That, however, might have been conscious humor on Tchaikowsky's part.

Katerina Geltzer made a great success yesterday afternoon. In the second act of the ballet, in which she made her first appearance, she seemed nervous, but in the third act she danced so brilliantly that she soon had the house in an uproar.

She is not very tall and rather lithe, although the lower parts of her legs have an unfortunate muscular development. Her face is piquant and always expressive and her body has been trained to suggest every emotion. Her technique is of a very high order. Her pirouette, for instance, is nothing short of astounding. She has a fine sense of humor, which is displayed on occasion, and also imagination, poetry, and intelligence. She seems to be more physical in her appeal than Pavlowa, and less delicate, not so mysteriously beautiful.

The comparison of the two inevitably brings to mind Taglioni and Fanny Elssler, and Miss Geltzer is more like the descriptions of the little Austrian.

Mr. Mordkin looked very wonderful and added greatly to the effect of the ballet, although he had very little dancing to do. The others were in the picture and assisted when necessary. Some of the dancing of the corps de ballet as swans was picturesque, especially at the close, where the waving fingers of the girls gave a wierd effect.

The scenery, painted by James Fox of the Metropolitan Opera House in emulation of the Russian impressionistic style, was very pleasant, indeed. Why are not more productions made along these simple lines? The costumes, especially those of the third act, were beautiful. The lighting was good, and so was the stage management, but the swans flying across the background were not very successful. It would, perhaps, be better to resort to a cinematograph for this effect. The orchestra, it must be confessed, played very badly.

After the ballet there were a series of divertissements. Alexander Volinine had a chance to show his facility in a classic dance, which he had previously exhibited at the Winter Garden when he appeared with Miss Gertrude Hoffmann's troupe. Bronislawa Pajitskaia, who in private life is Mrs. Mikail Mordkin, was seen in a visualized conception of *Anitra's Dance,* from the *Peer Gynt* suite.

But almost the *clou* of the afternoon was the wonderful dancing of Katerina Geltzer and Mikail Mordkin in a number simply called *Etude.* This dance, which included a little touch of bacchanale, was irresistible, and is likely to be given countless repetitions during Miss Geltzer's brief stay in New York.

—*The New York Times,* December 20, 1911

1. *Le Lac des Cygnes*: In later years this title was applied only to the Second Act of *Swan Lake*, but in 1911 it meant the four act version. / *Editor*
2. The same as Catherine Geltzer. / *Editor*

Igor Strawinsky

In America we are not accustomed to look to performances of the ballet, which, after all, is not an institution with us, for musical manna. There have doubtless been ballets given here with music by composers whose names occur in Grove's Dictionary, sometimes performed by a fairly good band, but we have not expected, or received, revelations on these occasions. Since the Russian Ballet (the organization directed by Serge de Diaghilew) has travelled to and fro in Europe, Paris, and more especially London, we have learned a thing or two in this respect. For much of the most interesting of the modern music has been brought to these cities by the Russians, who include not only ballet but also opera in their répertoire. They are responsible for the productions, outside of Russia, of Moussorgsky's two operas, *Boris Godunow* and *La Khovanchina* (this latter music-drama was not produced by the Imperial Theatres in Russia until over twenty years after its publication in the Rimsky-Korsakow version. Its presentation at Moscow took place after its Paris and London performances, and at Petrograd only a month or so before!); Rimsky-Korsakow's operas, *Ivan the Terrible*, *A Night in May*, and *The Golden Cock;* and Borodine's *Prince Igor*. As for ballets, Richard Strauss wrote *The Legend of Joseph* for these dancers; Maurice· Ravel, *Daphnis et Chloë;* Debussy, *Jeux;* Reynaldo Hahn, *Le Dieu Bleu;* Paul Dukas, *La Péri* (to be sure, this work was finally produced under other auspices; withdrawn by the composer from the Russians a few days before the date set for the first performance, on the ground that insufficient time had been allotted for rehearsals); and Tcherepnine, *Narcisse* and *Le Pavilion d'Armide;* but most important of all are the three ballets (and the lyric drama) contributed by Igor Strawinsky, who has, in a sense, developed a new medium out of the orchestra by writing a new language for it, although it may be plainly seen that he is the logical decendant of the really Russian composers (brushing aside the Tschaikowsky – Rubinstein interlude; nationalism was, of course, no object with these musicians). There are suggestions of Strawinsky's style so far back as Glinka, in the Oriental dances of *Russlan and Ludmilla*. You will find the germs of his method in Borodine's symphonies; from Moussorgsky to Strawinsky is but a step, especially if you refer to the original text of *Boris Godunow* and not the Rimsky-Korsakow version. In fact, Strawinsky, in spite of his radical departures from academic methods, is the inevitable defender of the faith of the famous "Five"[1] whose slogan was "Nationalism and Truth." As all real progress in art is dependent, in a measure, on the past, it is necessary to establish this fact.

My personal impressions of this young Russian's music and its effects on me are very strong. I attended the first performance in Paris[2] of Strawinsky's anarchistic (against the canons of academic art) ballet, *The Sacrifice to the Spring,* in which primitive emotions are both depicted and aroused by a dependence on barbarous rhythm, in which melody and harmony, as even so late a composer as Richard Strauss understands them, do not enter. A certain part of the audience, thrilled by what it considered a blasphemous attempt to destroy music as an art, and swept away with wrath, began very soon after the rise of the curtain to whistle, to make cat-calls, and to offer audible suggestions as to how the performance should proceed. Others of us, who liked the music and felt that the principles of free speech were at stake, bellowed defiance. It was war over art for the rest of the evening and the orchestra played on unheard, except occasionally when a slight lull occurred. The figures on the stage danced in time to music they had to imagine they heard and beautifully out of rhythm with the uproar in the auditorium. I was sitting in a box in which I had rented one seat. Three ladies sat in front of me and a young man occupied the place behind me. He stood up during the course of the ballet to enable himself to see more clearly. The intense excitement under which he was laboring, thanks to the potent force of the music, betrayed itself presently when he began to beat rhythmically on the top of my head with his fists. My emotion was so great that I did not feel the blows for some time. They were perfectly synchronized with the beat of the music. When I did, I turned around. His apology was sincere. We had both been carried beyond ourselves. Later, when the public's attitude had assumed a more formal aspect, I had a better opportunity for studying the score of this ballet.

My second personal impression is a memory of an evening a few nights later, when I attended a performance of Strawinsky's earlier ballet, *Petrouchka.*[3] *Petrouchka* is another kind of entertainment. It was a success with the public from the beginning, and is still an important feature in the répertoire of the Russian Ballet. It is by *Petrouchka*, in fact, that Strawinsky will be introduced to New York by

109

the Russians during the current season.... The curtains had closed on these pathetic scenes from the Russian carnival. They were drawn back to disclose Karsavina and Nijinsky. Presently a third figure appeared, very thin and short, with a Jewish profile (I do not know, however, that Strawinsky is a Jew). Dragged on the stage by Nijinsky, pale, awkward, and timid, his near-sighted eyes blinded by the footlights, the composer bowed his acknowledgements to the applause, nervously fingering his eyeglasses. This account would be incomplete without a reference to his dress, as irreproachable in fit and texture as that of Arturo Toscanini.

A London experience is also worth the telling. It happened after the first performance there of *The Nightingale*, a lyric drama to set a pace in the race towards the future. There was a long intermission after this short opera before the continuation of the bill, which included a performance of *The Legend of Joseph,* the composer himself conducting, and Steinberg's *Midas*. In the foyer I met my friend Alfred Hertz. Those who know this conductor are familiar with his moods. Tired, after a rehearsal of *Parsifal,* or excited before the performance of a work which he is about to conduct for the first time, he becomes *distrait* and unconversational to a degree which would not seem possible in a man who ordinarily is as fond of anecdote as he is of Viennese pastry. I recognized his mood on this occasion. Mopping his brow (it was June), he was good enough to explain.

"I can't stay here any longer," he said. "It's very embarrassing. Strauss asked me to come. I am here as his guest to hear *The Legend of Joseph,* but I can't listen to it. I'm too tired — I am exhausted. I have never heard such extraordinary music. I have never been so moved, so excited before at the performance of a new opera.... Oh, if I could have the privilege of introducing that work to New York, then I should be happy!"

I am very glad to quote these words to the lasting honor of one who realized at once the pleasure that Strawinsky's music, quite in a new mode, would give to the coming generation, and to a few in the present.

. . .An incident occurred which considerably changed the young composer's outlook, and which brought him to the attention of a larger world. He was "discovered" by the director of the Russian Ballet, Serge de Diaghilew, and commissioned to write a ballet on a Russian folk-story scenario fashioned by Michel Fokine. Leon Bakst and Golovine, the painters, completed the collaboration. The work, *The Firebird,* was terminated May 18, 1910, and produced three weeks later. The first sketches for this ballet must have been written before the death of Rimsky-Korsakow, if we are to believe a very delightful story told somewhere by Calvocoressi. On hearing Strawinsky play some bars of *The Firebird,* the older composer is quoted as saying: "Look here, stop playing that horrid thing; otherwise I might begin to enjoy it!" The production of *The Firebird* established the composer's reputation in Paris, and the very impressionists whose methods he has dubbed "hypocritical" were among the first to sign themselves his admirers. Of these Maurice Ravel was the leader. *Petrouchka* was completed just a year later (May 26, 1911), and its production by the Russian Ballet gave his fame a firm hold with the public. His third choreographic drama, *The Sacrifice to the Spring,* followed in 1913, and his opera, *The Nightingale,* in 1914. Several songs, including *Le petit Myosotis* and *Le Pigeon,* are other products of recent years.

It is astonishing to learn that *The Nightingale* was begun so early in the composer's career, but it is still more astonishing to discover that the first sketches of *The Sacrifice to the Spring* were written before *Petrouchka* was conceived. That ballet, which achieved the great honor of being hissed in Paris (I have described the incident earlier in this article), is the work on which, with *The Nightingale,* rests his chief claim to being a composer with something new to say. The work differs from most of the mimed dramas given by the Russians in that it is practically without a fable. The scenes take place in barbaric Russia, long before the Christian era, and we are introduced to rites connected with the worship of the soil and the springtide; after a series of ritual dances, one of the younger maidens is chosen as a sacrifice to the spring, whereupon she spares her friends the trouble of killing her by dancing herself to death. This exceedingly angular dance, the expression of religious hysteria, marvelously conceived by Nijinsky and thrice marvelously carried out by Mlle. Piltz, was one of the causes for the outbreaks at the early performances of the ballet.

The lack of a fable, the early and uncertain setting of the action, offered Strawinsky an opportunity which he seized with avidity. The music is not descriptive, it is rhythmical. All rhythms are beaten into the ears, one after another, and sometimes with complexities which seem decidedly unrhythmic on paper, but when carried out in performance assume a regularity of beat which a simple four-four time could not equal. H.E. Krehbiel, in his valuable book, *Afro-American Folksongs,* describes the tremendous effect made on him by the intricate rhythms (which he tried in vain to note down) of the musicians of African tribes at the World's Fair in Chicago (1893). The rhythmic effect of *The Sacrifice to the Spring* is as powerful and complex. It is interesting to remember, in this connection, that the ancient Greeks accorded rhythm a higher place than either melody or harmony. Strawinsky describes the dawn of a spring morning in a few measures at the beginning of the preludes (here, it must be admitted, there is a startling reminder of *l'Après-midi d'un Faune*), and then he settles down to the business, and art, of providing material for dances. This he has done with consummate effect. In many cases his chord formations could not be described in academic terms; the instruments employed add to the strangeness of the sounds. I remember one passage in which the entire corps of dancers is engaged in shivering, trembling from head to toe, to music which trembles also. It makes my flesh creep even to think of it again. At the beginning of the ballet the adolescents pound the earth with their feet, while a little old woman runs in and out between their legs, to the reiterated beat of a chord of F flat, A flat, C flat, F flat; G, B flat, D flat, and E flat, all in the bass (begin from below and read in order), while an occasional flute or a piccolo screams its way in high treble. Try this on your piano. "He has had recourse," writes Edward Burlingham Hill, "to a violently revolutionary style which is difficult to reduce to a systematic analysis. Chords employing minor and major triads simultaneously in different octaves, figures in double thirds, strange aggregations of notes that can hardly be described as chords, even with critical license, are the ingredients of this unusual style." M. Montague-Nathan, in his *Short History of Russian Music,* says: "In criticising the work, the mistake was made of suggesting that Strawinsky's music had gone back to an elemental stage in an endeavor to provide an appropriate setting for the pre-historic. In reality, of course, the movement was forward, in that music was used in a sphere to which it had hitherto been strange. That is progress. A composer who sets *The Creation* to living music is just as progressive as another who takes *The Last Judgement* as his theme."

Strawinsky seems to meet his problems according to their nature with an inevitable sense of the fitness of things. He has set, in *Petrouchka,* a story of the Russian fair; the leading characters are puppets; the period, 1830. The music is realistic in tone, in some instances intentionally vulgar. It has been pointed out that the themes of the nurses' dance, the dance of the *cochers,* and the Russian dance in the first scene, are founded on Russian folk-tunes. There is all through the piece an implied tone of a village carnival; the accordion and hurdy-gurdy are never very far away, in suggestion at least. The dancer, personified by Mme. Karsavina, trips her lightest measures to the fanfare of a cornet, and Petrouchka sobs out his heart to the empty sky to the screaming of a piccolo. There are tunes, real tunes, the piece abounds in them, and the whole is wrapped in an atmosphere of realism and truth which gives music the tone of originality. Incidentally, there is a triangle solo in the score.

M. Montagu-Nathan says: "The carnival music is a sheer joy, and the incidents making a demand upon music as a descriptive medium have been treated not merely with marvelous skill but with unfailing instinct for the true satiric touch. *Petrouchka* is, in fact, the musical presentment of Russian fantastic humor in the second generation. There is none of the heavy scoring once thought necessary to reveal the humorous possibilities of some particular situation; Strawinsky lives in a world which has learned to take things for granted, and his method is elliptical. This perception of proportion in humor is one of the surest indications of refinement, and *Petrouchka* not only testifies to the composer's possession of this quality, but provides an assurance that he has a technical equipment which can hardly betray him."

The fable is one of love and hate in that fanciful domain in which we become aware of the existence of a soul hitherto considered absent from such a corporeal habitation. Among the mingled crowd of merry-makers and mountebanks at the carnival is a showman, practiced in the black arts. In his booth he exposes his animated dolls: the dancer, flanked by Petrouchka, the simple fool, and the fierce Moor. The three enact a tragedy of jealousy which terminates in the "shedding of Petrouchka's vital sawdust."

The Firebird stirred another cell in the imagination of this young Russian giant. Again he is dealing with a Russian folk-tale, but it is a fairy story this time, not a vulgar story of country life; he has manipulated his orchestra into a thousand gorgeous colors to illustrate it. The instruments revolve their tones kaleidoscopically, reflecting the myriad hues with which Golovine and Bakst have invested the scene. The rhythms are exotic; the harmonies and melodies of the utmost brilliancy. One of the dances of the Firebird has a haunting melancholy about it which seems to have been wafted from the steppes.

The Firebird in the beginning of the action falls a prey to the young Prince Ivan; as the price of her freedom she offers him one of her plumes, which he accepts while she flies away into the soft blue shadows of the night. Dawn breaks, and Ivan finds himself in front of a magic castle, from the gates of which troop out a group of white-robed maidens. They indicate by means of their leader, Tsarevna, with whom Ivan at once falls in love, that he must not venture inside, but as soon as they have left him he rashly pushes back the great gate in front of him. There is a crash and in a moment out rushes pell-mell a huddled mass of slaves, dancers, men in armor, and buffoons, who surround him and drive him dizzy with their chatter. The uproar works up to a *crescendo* of frenzy when the monstrous figure of Kostchei, the Immortal, the lord of the castle, stalks out to quell the din. Kostchei has already turned others into stone, but over Ivan he has no power; the Firebird's plume protects him, and on his brandishing it before the terror-stricken god the bird herself appears. At first she makes the crowd dance; then she lulls them to sleep and shows Ivan where the egg containing Kostchei's soul is concealed. He brings it out and smashes it. The old god crumbles to pieces, the stones are brought to life, and the lovers' hands are joined. The character of Kostchei is an important one in Russian folk-lore; he is the subject of an opera by Rimsky-Korsakow. Ralston, in his *Russian Folk-Tales,* thus describes him: "Kostchei is merely one of the many incarnations of the dark spirit. . . . Sometimes he is described as altogether serpent-like in form; sometimes he seems to be a mixed nature, partly human and partly ophidian; but in some stories he is apparently framed after the fashion of a man. . . . He is called 'immortal' or 'deathless' because of his superiority to the ordinary laws of existence. . . . Sometimes his 'death' — that is, the object with which his life is indisputably connected — does not exist within his body." It may be seen that in almost every instance Strawinsky has followed the lead of the "Five" in choosing material closely associated with Russian folklore.[4]

(*August 6, 1915*)

— From "Igor Strawinsky: A New Composer," in *Music After the Great War*, Schirmer, 1915

1. "Five:" Cui, Borodine, Rimsky-Korsakow, Balakirew, and Moussorgsky. / *Editor*
2. *Sacrifice to the Spring:* Van Vechten calls the ballet by this name in his original article; it is, of course, *Le Sacre du Printemps* or *The Rite of Spring*. The Paris premiere which Van Vechten attended was May 29, 1913. There have been many interesting and curious versions of this and following performances of this ballet in its early history. One of the most enchanting is Gertrude Stein's version in her *Autobiography of Alice B. Toklas* (1933). She attended the second performance and shared her box with Van Vechten whom she did not know at the time. She was so impressed by him she composed a word "portrait" of him calling it *One* upon arriving home that night. Through unrelated incidents, she met him a week later when he was a guest at her Salon. It was the beginning of an enduring friendship that ended only with her death in 1946. / *Editor*
3. *Petrouchka:* An extensive and illustrated article on the ballet and its history and showing its grand revival is to be found in *Dance Magazine*, February, 1970. Extensive coverage of the revival is in *Dance News* magazine for March, 1970. / *Editor*
4. Stravinsky's work with Balanchine is outlined in an illustrated article in *Dance Magazine*, June, 1973. As a memorial to the composer, who died on April 8, 1971, the New York City Ballet held a Stravinsky Festival in June, 1972. *Dance Magazine* in its September, 1972, issue covers the event in text and photographs. / *Editor*

Stage Decoration As A Fine Art

Genius, even unclothed genius, is at all times preferable to mediocrity decked in gauds, but genius properly caparisoned is only added to...Let us take, for instance, the case of the Russian dancers. Anna Pavlowa is generally regarded as the greatest of living women dancers. A similar place is assigned Waslav Nijinsky among the male dancers. And yet it cannot be said that Mlle. Pavlowa, with her mediocre (in most instances) scenic and choreographic accompaniments, makes the effect that Nijinsky does surrounded by the Bakst scenery and the elemental spontaneity of the superb Russian ballet. Mlle. Pavlowa's genius creates the utmost enthusiasm; it awakens admiration on every hand; but it would be more compelling were it encased in the beauty which it suggests.

. . . Leon Bakst, who has designed many of the famous ballets which the Russians give in Paris and other Continental cities from time to time, proceeds on a lavish scale. There are no plastic features in a scene by Bakst. Everything is painted on flat canvas, but the barbaric gorgeousness, the impressionistic and suggestive qualities, appeal to the eye as no attempted copy of a real scene could ever do. The number of colors he uses in one scene is almost countless, and yet the combination is always thrilling and effective.

Bakst is better known for his *Sheherazade* than any other of his ballets, but he also designed the scenery for *Carnaval, Thamar, Jeux, Daphnis et Chloë, Narcisse, l'Après-midi d'un Faune,* and *Le Spectre de la Rose.*

He has further utilized his supreme talent for decoration in staging the dramas in which that Russian mime, Ida Rubinstein, has appeared at the Théâtre du Châtelet in Paris during recent seasons: Oscar Wilde's *Salome,* Verhaeren's *Hélène de Sparte,* and d'Annunzio's *Le Martyre de Saint-Sébastien,* and *La Pisanelle, ou la Mort parfumée.*

It was in this last play, produced in Paris in the spring of 1913 for ten special performances, that Bakst expressed himself perhaps more personally then he had hitherto been able to do. Unlimited means were placed at his disposal. He had all the money he wanted and an exactitude in color, in scene and costume, was aimed at which required the dyeing and redyeing of many stuffs, and the searching through countless shops for others.

The scene in the port, with the ship of the blood-red sails painted against a sky of blood-red clouds, in front of which figures garbed in scarlet, vermillion, maroon, rose, mulberry, carnation, and other shades of this brilliant color carried on the drama, will not be soon forgotten by those who saw it. In the final scene Bakst combined black, white, green, orange, rose, and magenta in the most extraordinary manner. In this play, too, he utilized a series of curtains of different colors, according to the scene, which hung half the depth of the stage on either side. And back of the proscenium arch, also on either side, was builded a column of gold, each column divided into numberless small pillars, like the mass which supports the ribs of a vaulted roof of a great Gothic cathedral.

This season Bakst has staged two new ballets for the Russians, Richard Strauss's *The Legend of Joseph,* in which Paolo Veronese is suggested in the superb Venetian robes, and *Papillons,* which calls into play the same qualities Bakst had already exhibited in his designs for *Carnaval.*

The new school of scene-painting in Russia is said to have been the inspiration of the painter Wronbel, who, however, did not do much himself, as he died before his ideas were fully accepted. Bakst, Alexandre Benois and N. Roerich took up the work. To Roerich we owe the *décors* of the ballet *The Sacrifice to the Spring,* devised by Nijinsky to carry out the ideas of the cubists, and which aroused storms of hisses whenever it was given in Paris. Alexandre Benois painted the scenes for *Petrouchka* and also those for *Le Pavilion d'Armide.* Serge Soudeikine is responsible for the decorations used in *La Tragédie de Salomé,* and Theodore Fedorowsky painted the extraordinary scenes for Moussorgsky's music drama, *La Khovanchina.* The costumes of the Persian ballet in this opera, of orange, with vivid patches of green and blue, rest in the memory. The art of the Russians, it seems to me, has found nearly complete expression. It is impossible for them to go much further in their violent riots of color, their barbaric impressionism.

It is a style particularly suited to the Russian Ballet performances; the effect makes a complete whole which those who have seen it cannot erase from the memory. Its practical application to other branches of theatrical entertainment is more difficult. Certain plays of Shakespeare could be dressed in this manner. Certainly *The Pirates of Penzance* and *Patience* would be superbly fitted by it; so would the music-dramas of Gluck, Wagner, and Richard Strauss. (*June, 1914*)

— Exerpted from *Music After the Great War,* Schirmer, 1915.

3

Alicia Markova

"Alicia Markova had elected to remain in her native element, the ether."

Queen Of The Dance

It is not difficult to recall the occasion (a certain evening in the Brooklyn Academy of Music) when I watched Anton Dolin actually seeming to *pull* his partner out of the air, while they were dancing the valse pas de deux in "Les Sylphides." Apparently Alicia Markova had elected to remain in her native element, the ether.

This is not the first, or the last, time that she has employed magic. Her stage life is a more or less continuous miracle; I remember specifically the beats in the second act of "Giselle," those nervous, hopping, entre-chats that always enchant the house, and the beautiful bent-over bourrées in "Rouge et Noir," less spectacular, but more moving. It has been said of some women that never a hair is out of place. Of Markova, one could say that never has an arm or a leg departed a quarter of an inch from perfection.

Naturally many attempts have been made to register this perfection, to describe this paragon's sense of style, her feather-like lightness, her infinite grace, her improbably beautiful line, and her most expressive emotional equipment. In 1935, Cyril Beaumont issued a slender volume on the subject in London, but at that early period a part of Markova had yet to be born and this book has long since been outdated. More recently, Agnes de Mille, another dancer, devoted an article to Markova. Brilliantly conceived and written, this paper purported to instruct the reader in the successive steps that lead to the making of a great dancer, but what emerged was a full-length portrait of the *greatest* dancer—an amazing piece of work, in which, nevertheless, several pertinent matters were scarcely touched upon. Very little is known, in America at any rate, concerning Markova's childhood, family life, and early dancing career. This deficiency has been partially atoned for by Anton Dolin, her former dancing partner, who has written an extended account consecrated to this dancer's personality and career.

Although Mr. Dolin has previously written and published several books about himself, he is better known as a dancing partner than in any other capacity. He is principally known, indeed, as the supporting partner of Alicia Markova. To put the matter still more succinctly, he is most frequently spoken of as the supporting partner of Alicia Markova in "Giselle." He remains, for the most part, the supporting partner in this new biographical essay. Standing modestly behind the ballerina, he takes only the most diffident bows, while she is permitted to curtsey. Occasionally, he lifts her to face the lights and the applause, awarding her his most fulsome praise. More often he dilates on the elegant turn of her ankle or the measureless beauty of her fluid arms.

Alicia Markova: Her Life And Art[1] is only biography in the conventional sense. The book lacks distinction and solidity. It is written guilelessly, with glaring omissions, if not too many distortions or actual misstatements of fact. Its breathless style is more suited to the medium of television than to the art of book-making.

Nevertheless, the principal figure emerges unscathed, as is her wont, under even more trying circumstances. If her complete portrait is not painted, at least the sketch is recognizable. After reading the book, one understands more fully Agnes de Mille's pregnant phrase regarding the ballerina: "She has been acclaimed the greatest dancer for just one reason: she intended to be."

The chapters about the school of Astafieva, about Alicia's mother and sisters, and especially the chapters about Guggy, the embarrassingly severe duenna, are largely fresh and bear internal evidence that they are true. Vincenzo Celli receives his just due for his important contribution in the way of coaching instruction in America. A vivid passage describes the occasion on which Sokolova discovered that Markova, the child, was bereft of the art of applying stage make-up. Choura Danilova emerges a charming figure, with her beautiful legs intact.

Author Dolin regards Kchessinska with wondering

admiration because she engaged Mischa Elman to play the *adagio* for her "Swan Lake," but old-time New Yorkers will remember that Mischa Elman frequently played the "Meditation " in *Thais* for Mary Garden's performances at the Manhattan Opera House. (On at least one occasion, if memory serves, Artur Rubinstein accompanied Markova's dancing on the piano.)

Olga Spessiva is never actually visible, but she is awarded several superlative paragraphs. Ninette de Valois and Lilian Baylis are permitted to appear in person and are more clearly defined. It is surprising that Diaghileff (Markova called him Sergy-pop) hardly seems to be here at all. His name occurs frequently, but he himself, never! Lucia Chase is barely mentioned and Sol Hurok is treated almost as shabbily.

Indeed, when Mr. Dolin writes about Markova's American career, he is most incomplete in his descriptions of her appearances with the Ballet Russe de Monte Carlo, and he gives us a similarly sketchy account of her years with the Ballet Theatre. As Dolin himself was in America during this extended period, his omissions are the more curious. I think the explanation is that this book was begun in leisure and completed in haste. The author, however, is categorically explicit in awarding America the palm as the country where Markova came of age artistically and to which she gave eight years of her greatest performances.

Mr. Dolin's book lacks both an index and a complete list of Markova's rôles with the dates when she first danced them. There are, however, many interesting and unusual illustrations.

— "Queen of the Dance," April 25, 1953 *The Saturday Review.*

1. *Alicia Markova: Her Life and Art.* by Anton Dolin. Hermitage House, 1953.

Gardenias For Alicia

It is not difficult for me to recall the occasion when I watched Anton Dolin seeming literally to pull his partner out of the air while they were negotiating the *valse pas de deux* in *Les Sylphides*. Apparently, Alicia Markova had elected to remain in her native element, the ether.[1]

Her stage life is a more or less continuous miracle, especially her unbroken astonishingly youthful appearance; the dazzling beats in the second act of *Giselle*, those nervous, hopping *entre-chats* which invariably enchant an audience, or the beautiful bent-over *bourrées* in *Rouge et Noir*, less spectacular, but more moving; her exit with flickering limbs in *Firebird*, or any moment at all of her young and tender Juliet. On one unforgotten evening, she stood on one point, literally one of her great toes, for so long a time, at the conclusion of the Rose Adagio in *The Sleeping Beauty*, that an ecstatic sigh of satisfaction rustled through the audience when she descended.

It has been said of Markova that never, under any circumstances or on any occasion, has a hair of her head been discovered out of place. It might be added that never has a leg or an arm departed a quarter of an inch from perfection. Naturally, many attempts have been made, more or less successfully, to capture the basis of this perfection, to describe this paragon's faultless sense of style, whatever the period of her impersonation, her featherlike lightness in elevation, her infinite grace, her improbably beautiful line, often a line broken for an effect, and her most expressive emotional equipment, her soulful visions, her dreams of interpretation, as manifested during her dancing. Perhaps, however, the quality which more than any other, singles her out from other ballerinas, is her ability to project with so much intensity.

When she first danced in New York in 1938, she was still, in some respects, a somewhat immature dancer. For years she had retained a feeling that no one in London could be the equal of Diaghilev's brilliant ballet-master Enrico Cecchetti, but in New York she was persuaded to work with Vincenzo Celli, and it was with his assistance that she hewed her way to the top rank of her profession. For an extended period he was her permanent coach. Every morning at eleven she practiced in his studio and he observed every one of her performances from a seat near the stage. His duties did not require him to express enthusiasm; the dancer paid him to note any fault of movement or posture, however slight. When she had achieved an impeccable technique, when she was no longer aware of faults for correction, it was possible for her to devote her complete attention, while dancing, to interpretation.

Markova's repertory is prodigious, although frequently limited by directorial zeal or what is known as public demand. Her remarkable memory keeps pace with her repertory. She is invariably willing to assist other dancers when they are willing to accept assistance. When a ballet that has lain dormant for years is finally restored to the repertory, she will recall details of movement with far more facility than the original choreographer can. Her versatility is unlimited. She dances classical or modern rôles with equal ease. She is at home in romantic tragedy and in comedy.

She has danced *Giselle* more frequently and more successfully than any other dancer of our time and her name usually accompanies any mention of this ballet. But many other rôles in her vast repertory are favorites with her public; *Pas de Quatre* with its mood of gentle travesty; *Orfeo,* the second act of which, laid in the Elysian Fields, she danced in soft shoes; *Aleko,* in which she suggested a priestess of evil, while other dancers in the rôle appeared to be portraying a prostitute; the tender youthfulness of *Juliet* with its renaissance style of gesture and movement, suggested by Florentine paintings; *Rouge et Noir,* a ballet of disembodied grief, in which her body, completely exposed in a leotard of black and white, devised by Matisse, exhibited her every movement as exquisite in line; *Romantic*

Age, a stupid ballet, in which she was able to display her unusually well-developed gift for comedy in the rôle of the nymph who could not dance, contrasting this side of the part with that of the same character at the conclusion, who now danced more entrancingly than any of her sister nymphs. This rôle eluded the efforts of other dancers who succeeded her in the part, apparently because they were unable to dance badly, so that there was no contrast between the beginning of the ballet and the close. I have never seen Markova in *Coppélia,* but I feel certain that she would be miraculously elflike in it. And how much I would like to watch her in the superb *grand pas de deux* in the last act!

Other periods have been celebrated for greater actors, greater painters, greater opera singers, and greater writers. In the age of our contemporary world, great violinists, great pianists and great dancers have flourished. The technique of the dancer and of the instrumentalists has advanced to a degree in which it is impossible for even a bad performer to make a public appearance unless he has solved most of the technical problems. This is not the day of the amateur. We in the United States, during the last twenty-five years, have been fortunate in having with us some of the greatest dancing talent the world has ever known. Probably only in the age of Taglioni was anything approaching it ever seen.

It is most generally conceded that Alicia Markova emerges at the top of the dancing perfection of the present age. I stand in not a little awe of that great lady's prowess and artistry. There may have been greater technicians, but I have not been aware of them. Naturally inspection of Taglioni was denied me, but I have seen Pavlova almost as many times as I have seen Markova. I have been told of dancers, unknown to the theatre, who were able to dash off forty-five *fouettés* with ease in the class-room. It is not merely technique which places Markova on the heights where she stands today. It is dedication, dedication to an ideal, to a dream, to the spirit of the dance. It is what she has inside her and her ability to project it that has given her her eminence.

It is no longer fashionable to unharness the horses from a ballerina's carriage so that we may draw it ourselves. However, we still have our hands with which to applaud, our tongues to speak approval, and our pens to inscribe it. It is my ambition to be able to permit future generations to learn that not only do some of us believe Markova to be the greatest figure on the contemporary dancing stage, but one of the greatest of all time. At this point, permit Agnes de Mille to speak:

"The press (for Markova) got better every year, until John Martin threw caution away: 'Not only the best living ballet dancer, but probably the greatest who ever lived.' One cannot go beyond this recognition. It is absolute." Miss de Mille continues: "She has been acclaimed the greatest ballet dancer for just one reason: she intended to be."

Permit me to quote a little more from the enthusiastic Mr. Martin: "Realizing that her strength lies in evocation rather than spectacle, in spirit rather than body, in distillations of the spirit rather than propulsions of force, she has concentrated with the intensity of a mystic upon these magic processes and eliminated every element that would deny or diminish them. If dancing can be disembodied, Markova's is in its present manifestation; of a sensitive and visually exquisite bodily instrument only its eloquence concerns her. Indeed, if she shears away one more material irrelevancy, she may vanish altogether. Such an art may not arouse the lusty *balletomanes* to bravos, but it is a phenomenon which at least one inveterate ballet-goer has never seen equalled."

Efrem Kurtz, who has conducted for both dancers, has written: "The music followed Pavlova, Markova follows the music".

Elsa Maxwell had a moment of inspiration when she said: "Why Markova is so wonderful is because you sense her, see her, but you don't touch her, you never hear her."

It has been my pleasure and my privilege during Markova's residence in America, and her series of visits here, to photograph her in color[2] in most of her celebrated rôles, and a few minor ones such as Camille or Iztepac. These films frequently have been projected on a screen for the enjoyment or instruction of many groups, including many dancers. I hope to be able to arrange my affairs so that these showings may continue indefinitely in order that future generations may learn a good deal about what Markova was really like. The dancer herself has always realized the importance of this perpetuation of her appearance, suggestions of her style of dancing, projections of her legs and arms alone, and has offered me every assistance in the making of these films. A photographic session of this character requires infinite patience, patience while backgrounds are being arranged, patience while the dancer decides exactly what moment she wishes to celebrate in a chain which offers an endless choice of moments; sometimes a half-hour is exhausted in a discussion of these matters. It is during these séances that I have learned to understand the complete dedication Markova offers to her work. She arrives for a "sitting" at least an hour before she goes before the lens, more frequently an hour and a half before, occupying her time in the arrangement of her hair, the application of her make-up, and in dressing. Her dresses have always been cleaned and pressed for such occasions; her ballet shoes are always pristine; her flesh-, ings unspotted. When, at last she is ready, and nothing can hurry her, she glides into the studio with a reassuring and somewhat shy smile, as if she were saying by her manner: "I have done my part as well as I know how; now you do *YOURS.*" All this and what follows is as fatiguing as a performance at the Metropolitan would be, perhaps more fatiguing. However, I recall her complaining only once, of the action of the sun on her feet during the outdoor photographing of her rôle in *Giselle*. Sometimes she arrives early in the afternoon, sometimes after a stage appearance, when she appears in her theatre costume, already in

make-up, but all this has to be tidied. Once, after such a late séance, she hesitated for an hour or so, so that she might cool off and eat the leg of a chicken, with salad, and slowly sip a glass of champagne. She left my apartment about 4 a.m. In the morning I learned that she was in a hospital. Although she had showed no signs of it here, in the night she had struggled with pain. She was removed to a hospital for an emergency operation in the morning, which kept her off the stage for several months. When she is in New York however, only such a catastrophe will prevent her from attending a showing of her pictures.
(*April, 1960*)

— Introduction to *Giselle and I* by Alicia Markova. Vanguard Press, 1960.

1. The reader will notice that the first paragraph of Van Vechten's book review on Anton Dolin's study of Markova, written in 1953, is very similar to the first paragraph and part of the second in his Introduction to Markova's autobiography, written in 1960. Whether this was accomplished on purpose by Van Vechten, perhaps because he *liked* the phrasing, or is a repetition for effect; whatever, it is a curious idea expressed in print seven years apart. / *Editor*
2. For readers who may not be acquainted with Van Vechten's many careers within careers, he was an avid photographer of persons in the arts, beginning in the early Thirties and lasting until his death in 1964. His photographic studies of dancers are justly famous and are housed in The Museum of Modern Art, New York. / *Editor*

4

Music and Dance on the Iberian Peninsula

"I love Miro, himself and his pictures. Once he escorted me and a friend all over Barcelona. I photographed him, dined with him several times and once danced the Sardanas with him and several Duchesses in the street."

(Quoted from a letter to me on January 17, 1963. / Editor)

The Land Of Joy

An idle observer of theatrical conditions might derive a certain ironic pleasure from remarking the contradiction implied in the professed admiration of the constables of the playhouse for the unconventional and their almost passionate adoration for the conventional. We constantly hear it said that the public cries for novelty, and just as constantly we see the same kind of acting, the same gestures, the same Julian Mitchellisms and George Marionisms and Ned Wayburnisms repeated in and out of season, summer and winter. Indeed, certain conventions (which bore us even now) are so deeply rooted in the soil of our theatre that I see no hope of their being eradicated before the year 1999, at which date other conventions will have supplanted them and will likewise have become tiresome.

In this respect our theatre does not differ materially from the theatres of other countries except in one particular. In Europe the juxtaposition of nations makes an interchange of conventions possible, which brings about slow change or rapid revolution. Paris, for example, has received visits from the Russian Ballet which almost assumed the proportions of Tartar invasions. London, too, has been invaded by the Russians and by the Irish. The Irish playwrights, indeed, are continually pounding away at British middle-class complacency. Germany, in turn, has been invaded by England (we regret that this sentence has only an artistic and figurative significance) (written in 1917 / *Editor*), and we find Max Reinhardt well on his way toward giving a complete cycle of the plays of Shakespeare; a few years ago we might have observed Deutschland grovelling hysterically before Oscar Wilde's *Salome,* a play which, at least without its musical dress, has not, I believe, even yet been performed publicly in London. In Italy, of course, there are no artistic invasions (nobody cares to pay for them) and even the conventions of the Italian theatre themselves, such as the *Commedia del'Arte,* are quite dead; so the country remains as dormant, artistically speaking, as a rag rug, until an enthusiast like Marinetti arises to take it between his teeth and shake it back into rags again.

Very often whisperings of art life in the foreign theatre (such as accounts of Stanislavski's accomplishments in Moscow) cross the Atlantic. Very often the husks of the realities (as was the case with the Russian Ballet) are imported. But whispers and husks have about as much influence as the "New York Times" in a mayoralty campaign, and as a result we find the American theatre as little aware of world activities in the drama as a deaf mute living on a pole in the desert of Sahara would be. Indeed any intrepid foreign investigator who wishes to study the American drama, American acting, and American stage decoration will find them in almost as virgin a condition as they were in the time of Lincoln.[1]

A few rude assaults have been made on this smug eupepsy. I might mention the coming of Paul Orleneff, who left Alla Nazimova with us to be eventually swallowed up in the conventional American theatre. Four or five years ago a company of Negro players at the Lafayette Theatre gave a performance of a musical revue that boomed like a big bell in the Kremlin at Moscow. Nobody could be deaf to the sounds. Florenz Ziegfeld took over as many of the tunes and gestures as he could buy for his *Follies* of that season, but he neglected to import the one essential quality of the entertainment, its style, for the exploitation of which Negro players were indispensable.[2] For the past two months Mimi Aguglia, one of the greatest actresses of the world, has been performing in a succession of classic and modern plays (a répertoire comprising dramas by Shakespeare, d'Annunzio, and Giacosa) at the Garibaldi Theatre, on East Fourth Street, before very large and very enthusiastic audiences, but uptown culture and management acumen will not awaken to the importance of this gesture until they read about it in some book published in 1950...[3]

All of which is merely by way of prelude to what I feel must be something in the nature of lyric outburst and verbal explosion. A few nights ago a Spanish company, unheralded, unsung, indeed almost unwelcomed by such reviewers as had to trudge to the out-of-the-way Park Theatre,[4] came to New York, in a musical revue entitled *The Land of Joy*. The score was written by Joaquin Valverde, *fils*, whose music is not unknown to us, and the company included La Argentina, a Spanish dancer who had given matinées here in a past season without arousing more than mild enthusiasm. The theatrical impressarii, the song publishers, and the Broadway rabble stayed away on the first night. It was all very well, they might have reasoned, to read about the goings on in Spain, but they would never do in America. Spanish dancers had been imported in the past without awakening undue excitement. Did not the great Carmencita herself visit America twenty or more years ago? These impressarii had ignored the existence of a great psychological (or more properly physiological) truth: you cannot mix Burgundy and Beer! One Spanish dancer surrounded by Americans is just as much lost as the great Nijinsky himself was in an English music hall, where he made a complete and dismal failure. And so they would have been very much astonished (had they been present) on the opening night to have witnessed all the scenes of uncontrollable enthusiasm — just as they are described by Havelock Ellis, Richard Ford, and Chabrier — repeated. The audience, indeed, became hysterical, and broke into wild cries of *Olé! Olé!* Hats were thrown on the stage. The audience became as abandoned as the players, became a part of the action.

You will find all this described in "The Soul of Spain," in "Gatherings from Spain," in Chabrier's letters,[5] and it had all been transplanted to New York almost without a whisper of preparation, which is fortunate, for if it had been expected, doubtless we would have found the way to spoil it. Fancy the average New York first-night audience, stiff and unbending, sceptical and sardonic, welcoming this exhibition! Havelock Ellis gives an ingenious explanation for the fact that Spanish dancing has seldom if ever successfully crossed the border of the Iberian peninsula: "The finest Spanish dancing is at once killed or degraded by the presence of an indifferent or unsympathetic public, and that is probably why it cannot be transplanted, but remains local." Fortunately the Spaniards in the first-night audience gave the cue, unlocked the lips and loosened the hands of us cold Americans. For my part, I was soon yelling *Olé!* louder than anybody else.

The dancer, Doloretes, is indeed extraordinary. The gipsy fascination, the abandoned, perverse bewitchery of this female devil of the dance is not to be described by mouth, typewriter, or quilled pen. Heine would have put her at the head of his dancing temptresses in his ballet of *Méphistophéla* (found by Lumley too indecent for representation at Her Majesty's Theatre, for which it was written; in spite of which the scenario was published in the repectable "Revue de Deux Mondes"). In this ballet a series of dancing celebrities is exhibited by the female Méphistophélès for the entertainment of her victim. After Salome had twisted her flanks and exploited the prowess of her abdominal muscles to perfunctory applause, Doloretes would have heated the blood, not only of Faust, but of the ladies and gentlemen in the orchestra stalls, with the clicking of her heels, the clacking of her castanets, now held high over head, now held low behind her back, the flashing of her ivory teeth, the shrill screaming, electric magenta of her smile, the wile of her wriggle, the passion of her performance. And close beside her the sinuous Mazantinita would flaunt a garish tambourine and wave a shrieking fan. All inanimate objects, shawls, mantillas, combs, and cymbals, become inflamed with life, once they are pressed into the service of these señoritas, languorous and forbidding, indifferent and sensuous. Against these rude gipsies the refined grace and Goyaesque elegance of La Argentina stand forth in high relief, La Argentina, in whose hands the castanets become as potent an instrument for our pleasure as the violin does in the fingers of Jascha Heifetz. Bilbao, too, with his thundering heels and his tauromachian gestures, bewilders our highly magnetized senses. When, in the dance, he pursues, without catching, the elusive Doloretes, it would seem that the limit of dynamic effects in the theatre has been reached.

Here are singers! The limpid and lovely soprano of the comparatively placid Maria Marco, who introduces figurations into the brilliant music she sings at every turn. One indecent (there is no other word for it) chromatic oriental phrase is so strange that none of us can ever recall it or forget it! And the frantically nervous Luisita Puchol, whose eyelids spring open like a cover of a Jack-in-the-box, and whose hands flutter like saucy butterflies, sings suggestive popular ditties just a shade better than any one else I know of.

But *The Land of Joy* does not rely on one or two principals for its effect. The organization as a whole is as full of fire and purpose as the original Russian Ballet; the costumes themselves, in their blazing, heated colours, constitute the ingredients of an orgy; the music, now sentimental (the adaptability of Valverde, who has lived in Paris, is little short of amazing; there is a vocal waltz in the style of Arditi that Mme. Patti might have introduced into the lesson scene of *Il Barbiere;* there is another song in the style of George M. Cohan — these by way of contrast to the Iberian music), now pulsing with rhythmic life, is the best Spanish music we have yet heard in this country. The whole entertainment, music, colours, costumes, songs, dances, and all, is as nicely arranged in its crescendos and decrescendos, its prestos and adagios as a Mozart finale. The close of the first act, in which the ladies sweep the stage with long ruffled trains, suggestive of all the Manet pictures you have ever seen, would seem to be unapproachable, but the most striking costumes and the wildest dancing are reserved for the very last scene of all. There these bewildering señoritas come forth in the splendorous envelope of embroidered Manila shawls, and such shawls!

Prehistoric African roses of unbelieveable measure decorate a texture of turquoise, from which depends nearly a yard of silken fringe. In others mingle royal purple and buff, orange and white, black and the kaleidoscope! The revue, a sublimated form of zarzuela, is calculated, indeed, to hold you in a dangerous state of nervous excitement during the entire evening, to keep you awake for the rest of the night, and to entice you to the theatre the next night and the next. It is as intoxicating as vodka, as insidious as cocaine, and it is likely to become a habit, like these stimulants. I have found, indeed, that it appeals to all classes of taste, from that of a telephone operator, whose usual artistic debauch is the latest antipyretic novel of Robert W. Chambers, to that of the frequenter of the concert halls.

I cannot resist further cataloguing; details shake their fists in my memory; for instance, the intricate rhythms of Valverde's elaborately syncopated music (not at all like ragtime syncopation), the thrilling orchestration (I remember one dance which is accompanied by drum taps and oboe, nothing else!), the utter absence of tangos (which are Argentine), and habaneras (which are Cuban), most of the music being written in two-four and three-four time, and the interesting use of folk-tunes; the casual and very suggestive indifference of the dancers, while they are not dancing, seemingly models for a dozen Zuloaga paintings, the apparently inexhaustible skill and variety of these dancers in action, winding ornaments around the melodies with their feet and bodies and arms and heads and castanets as coloratura sopranos do with their voices. Sometimes castanets are not used; cymbals supplant them, or tambourines, or even fingers. Once, by some esoteric witchcraft, the dancers seemed to tap upon their arms. The effect was so stupendous and terrifying that I could not project myself into that aloof state of mind necessary for a calm dissection of its technique.

What we have been thinking of all these years in accepting the imitation and ignoring the actuality I don't know; it has all been down in black and white. What

Richard Ford saw and wrote down in 1846 I am seeing and writing down in 1917.[6] How these devilish Spaniards have been able to keep it up all this time I can't imagine. Here we have our paradox. Spain has changed so little that Ford's book is still the best to be procured on the subject (you may spend many a delightful half-hour with the charming irony of its pages for company). Spanish dancing is apparently what it was a hundred years ago; no wind from the north has disturbed it. Stranger still, it depends for its effect on the acquirement of a brilliant technique. Merely to play the castanets requires a severe tutelage. And yet it is all as spontaneous, as fresh, as unstudied, as vehement in its appeal, even to Spaniards, as it was in the beginning. Let us hope that Spain will have no artistic reawakening.

Aristotle and Havelock Ellis and Louis Sherwin have taught us that the theatre should be an outlet for suppressed desires. So, indeed, the ideal theatre should. As a matter of fact, in most playhouses (I will generously refrain from naming the one I visited yesterday) I am continually suppressing a desire to strangle somebody or other, but after a visit to the Spaniards I walk out into Columbus Circle completely purged of pity and fear, love, hate, and all the rest. It is an experience.
(*November 3, 1917*)

— From *The Music of Spain*, Knopf, 1918.

1. Van Vechten was writing before the period of the Provincetown Players, the Theatre Guild, the Group Theatre and other superior companies who were active in the two decades following his article. / *Editor*
2. See chapter on "The Negro Theatre" for more detailed account. / *Editor*
3. Van Vechten was correct in his theory concerning the apathy of theatre management and critics towards certain theatrical enterprise, but he was unfortunate in his choice of an interpreter, Mimi Aguglia, who's fame has not survived her. / *Editor*
4. The Park Theatre was located at 59th Street and Broadway, considerably off-center for the theatre district in 1917, but today very

141

near the Lincoln Center complex. / *Editor*
5. See chapter *Spain and Music* for extensive coverage. / *Editor*
6. Richard Ford, 1796-1858. English author, who published *A Handbook For Travellers In Spain.* / *Editor*

Spain and Music

All the world dances in Spain, at least it would seem so, in reading over the books of the Marco Polos who have made voyages of discovery on the Iberian peninsula. Guitars seem to be as common there as pea-shooters in New England, and strumming seems to set the feet a-tapping and voices a-singing, what, they care not. (Havelock Ellis says: "It is not always agreeable to the Spaniard to find that dancing is regarded by the foreigner as a peculiar and important Spanish institution. Even Valera, with his wide culture, could not escape this feeling; in a review of a book about Spain by an American author entitled 'The Land of the Castanet' — a book which he recognized as full of appreciation for Spain — Valera resented the title. It is, he says, as though a book about the United States should be called 'The Land of Bacon.' ") Oriental colour is streaked through and through the melodies and harmonies, many of which betray their Arabian origin; others are *flamenco,* or gipsy. The dances, almost invariably accompanied by song, are generally in 3/4 time or its variants such as 6/8 or 3/8; the tango, of course, is in 2/4. But the dancers evolve the most elaborate inter-rhythms out of these single measures, creating thereby a complexity of effect which defies any comprehensible notation on paper. As it is on this *fioritura,* if I may be permitted to use the word in this connection, of the dancer that the sophisticated composer bases some of his most natural and national effects, I shall linger on the subject. La Argentina has re-arranged many of the Spanish dances for purposes of the concert stage, but in her translation she has retained in a large measure this interesting complication of rhythm, marking the irregularity of the beat, now with a singularly complicated detonation of heel-tapping now with a sudden bend of a knee, now with the subtle quiver of an eye-lash, now with a shower of castanet sparks (an instrument which requires a hard tutelage for its complete mastery; Richard Ford tells us that even the children in the streets of Spain rap shells together, to become self-taught artists in the use of it).

Probably Pastora Imperio is the foremost of all contemporary Spanish dancers. She is a gipsy, the daughter of the dancer, La Mejorana, and Victor Rojes, a tailor to bull-fighters, and she married the *torero,* El Gallo. She made her début at the Japonés, the best variety theatre in Madrid, opened in 1900. In 1902 she went to the Novedadés in the Calle Alcala, where La Argentina, then known as Aidá, and the famous Amalia Molina first appeared in Madrid. The Brothers Quintero have inscribed a sonnet to Pastora Imperio and they wrote their "Historia de Sevilla" for her use. Julio Romero de Torres has painted her. And Benavente, himself, the greatest, perhaps, of modern Spanish writers, has written a description of her dancing: "Her flesh burns with the consuming heat of all eternity, but her body is like the very pillar of the sanctuary, palpitating as it is kindled in the glow of sacred fires. . .Watching Pastora Imperio life becomes more intense. The loves and hates of other worlds pass before our eyes and we feel ourselves heroes, bandits, hermits assailed by temptation, shameless bullies of the tavern — whatever is highest and lowest in one. A desire to shout out horrible things takes possession of us: *Gitanaza!* Thief! Assassin! Then we turn to curse. Finally, summing it all up, in a burst of exaltation we praise God, because we believe in God while we look at Pastora Imperio, just as we do when we read Shakespeare." Recently La Imperio has been appearing in a one act piece, the music of which was arranged from de Falla's *El Amor Brujo.*

Amalia Molina, mentioned above, was in her prime ten years or so ago...Zuloaga has painted several portraits of Anita Ramirez and other Spanish dancers. One of his most admired pictures is of a gipsy dancer in *torero* costume. Here, too, I may speak of La Goya, a delightful music-hall singer who has won fame not only in Spain but in South America as well. She has made a special study of costumes. Of a more popular type, but not more of a favourite, is Raquel Meller.

Chabrier, in his visit to Spain with his wife in 1882, attempted to note down some of these rhythmic variations achieved by the dancers while the musicians strummed their guitars, and he was partially successful. But all in all he only succeeded in giving in a single measure each variation; he did not attempt to weave them into the intricate pattern which the Spanish women contrive to make of them.

There is a singular similarity to be observed between this heel-tapping and the complicated drum-tapping of the African negroes of certain tribes. In his book "Afro-American Folksongs," H.E. Krehbiel thus describes the musical accompaniment of the dances in the Dahoman Village at the World's Columbian Exposition in Chicago (1893): "These dances were accompanied by choral song and the rhythmical and harmonious beating of drums and bells, the song being in unison. The harmony was a tonic major triad broken up rhythmically in a most intricate and amazingly ingenious manner. The instruments were tuned with excellent justness. The fundamental tone came from a drum made of a hallowed log about three feet long with a single head, played by one who seemed to be the leader of the band, though there was no giving of signals. The drum was beaten with the palms of the hands. A variety of smaller drums, some with one, some with two heads, were beaten variously with sticks and fingers. The bells, four in number, were of iron and were held mouth upward and struck with sticks. The players showed the most remarkable rhythmical sense and skill that ever came under my notice. Berlioz in his supremest effort with his army of drummers produced nothing to compare in artistic interest with the harmonious drumming of these savages. The fundamental effect was a combination of double and triple time, the former kept by the singers, the latter by the drummers, but it is impossible to convey the idea of the wealth of detail achieved by the drummers by means of exchange of the rhythms, syncopation of both simultaneously, and dynamic devices. Only by making a score of the music could this have been done. I attempted to make such a score by enlisting the help of the late John C. Filmore, experienced in Indian music, but we were thwarted by the players who, evidently divining our purpose when we took out our notebooks, mischievously changed their manner of playing as soon as we touched pencil to paper."

The resemblance between negro and Spanish music is very noticeable. Mr. Krehbiel says that in South America Spanish melody has been imposed on negro rhythm. In the dances of the people of Spain, as Chabrier points out, the melody is often practically nil; the effect is rhythmic (an effect which is emphasized by the obvious harmonic and melodic limitations of the guitar, which invariably accompanies all singers and dancers). If there were a melody or if the guitarists played well (which they usually do not) one could not distinguish its contours what with the cries of *Ole!* and the heel-beats of the performers. Spanish melodies, indeed, are often scraps of tunes, like the African Negro melodies. The habanera is a true African dance, taken to Spain by way of Cuba, as Albert Friedenthal points out in his book, "Musik, Tanz, und Dichtung bei den Kreolen Amerikas." Whoever was responsible, Arab, Negro, or Moor (Havelock Ellis says that the dances of Spain are closely allied with the ancient dances of Greece and Egypt), the Spanish dances betray their oriental origin in their complexity of rhythm (a complexity not at all obvious on the printed page, as so much of it depends on dancer, guitarist, singer, and even public!), and the *fioriture* which decorate their melody when melody occurs. While

Spanish religious music is perhaps not distinctively Spanish, the dances invariably display marked national characteristics; it is on these, then (some in greater, some in less degree), that the composers in and out of Spain have built their most atmospheric inspirations, their best pictures of popular life in the Iberian peninsula. A good deal of the interest of this music is due to the important part the guitar plays in its construction; the modulations are often contrary to all rules of harmony and (yet, some would say) the music seems to be effervescent with variety and fire. Of the guitarists Richard Ford ("Gatherings from Spain," published in London in 1851) says: "The performers seldom are very scientific musicians; they content themselves with striking the chords, sweeping the whole hand over the strings, or flourishing, and tapping the board with the thumb, at which they are very expert. Occasionally in the towns there is some one who has attained more power over this ungrateful instrument; but the attempt is a failure. The guitar responds coldly to Italian words and elaborate melody, which never come home to Spanish ears or hearts." (An exception must be made in the case of Miguel Llobet. I first heard him play at Pitts Sanborn's concert at the Punch and Judy Theatre (April 17, 1916) for the benefit of Hospital 28 in Bourges, France, and he made a deep impression on me. In one of his numbers, the *Spanish Fantasy* of Farrega, he astounded and thrilled me. He seemed at all times to exceed the capacity of his instrument, obtaining a variety of colour which was truly amazing. In this particular number he not only plucked the keyboard but the fingerboard as well, in intricate and rapid *tempo;* seemingly two different kinds of instruments were playing. But at all times he variated his tone; sometimes he made the instrument sound almost as though it had been played by wind and not plucked. Especially did I note a suggestion of the bagpipe. A true artist. None of the music, the fantasy mentioned, a serenade of Albéniz, and a Menuet of Tor, was particularly interesting, although the Fantasia contained some fascinating references to folk-dance tunes.

There is nothing sensational about Llobet, a quiet prim sort of man; he sits quietly in his chair and makes music. It might be a harp or a 'cello — no striving for personal effect.)

The Spanish dances are infinite in number and for centuries back they seem to form part and parcel of Spanish life. Discussion as to how they are danced is a feature of the descriptions. No two authors agree, it would seem; to a mere annotator the fact is evident that they are danced differently on different occasions. It is obvious that they are danced differently in different provinces. The Spaniards, as Richard Ford points out, are not too willing to give information to strangers, frequently because they themselves lack the knowledge. Their statements are often misleading, sometimes intentionally so. They do not understand the historical temperament. Until recently many of the art treasures and archives of the peninsula were but poorly kept. Those who lived in the shadow of the Alhambra admired only its shade. It may be imagined that there has been even less interest displayed in recording the folk-dances. "Dancing in Spain is now a matter which few know anything about," writes Havelock Ellis, "because every one takes it for granted that he knows all about it; and any question on the subject receives a very ready answer which is usually of questionable correctness." Of the music of the dances we have many records, and that they are generally in 3/4 time or its variants we may be certain. As to whether they are danced by two women, a woman and a man, or a woman alone, the authorities do not always agree. The confusion is added to by the oracular attitude of the scribes. It seems quite certain to me that this procedure varies. That the animated picture almost invariably possesses great fascination there are only too many witnesses to prove. I myself can testify to the marvel of some of them, set to be sure in strange frames, the Feria in Paris, for example; but even without the surroundings, which Spanish dances demand, the diablerie, the shivering intensity of these fleshly women, always wound tight with such shawls as only the mistresses of kings might wear in other countries, have drawn taut the *real thrill.* It is dancing which enlists the co-operation not only of the feet and legs, but of the arms, and, in fact, the entire body.

The smart world in Spain today dances much as the smart world does anywhere else, although it does not, I am told, hold a brief for our tango, which Mr. Krehbiel suggests is a corruption of the original African habanera. But in older days many of the dances, such as the pavana, the sarabande, and the gallarda, were danced at the court and were in favour with the nobility. (Although presumably of Italian origin, the pavana and gallarda were more popular in Spain than in Rome. Fuertes says that the sarabande was invented in the middle of the sixteenth century by a dancer called Zarabanda who was a native of either Seville or Guayaquil.) The pavana, an ancient dance of grave and stately measure, was much in vogue in the sixteenth and seventeenth centuries. An explanation of its name is that the figures executed by the dancers bore a resemblance to the semi-circular wheel-like spreading of the tail of a peacock. In Catulle Mendés's song, *La Pavana,* set to music by Alfred Bruneau, he compares the pavane to a peacock. The gallarda (French, gaillard) was usually danced as a relief to the pavana (and indeed often follows it in the dance-suites of the classical composers in which these forms all figure). The jacara, or more properly xacara, of the sixteenth century, was danced in accompaniment to a romantic, swashbuckling ditty. The Spanish folias were a set of dances danced to a simple tune treated in a variety of styles with very free accompaniment of castanets and bursts of song. Corelli in Rome in 1700 published twenty-four variations in this form, which have been played in our day by Fritz Kreisler and other violinists.

The names of the modern Spanish dances are often confused in the descriptions offered by observing travellers, for the reasons already noted. Hundreds of these descriptions exist, and it is difficult to choose the most telling of them. Gertrude Stein, who has spent the last two years in

Spain, has noted the rhythm of several of these dances by the mingling of her original use of words with the ingratiating medium of *vers libre*. She has succeeded, I think, better than some musicians in suggesting the intricacies of the rhythm. I should like to transcribe one of these attempts here, but that I have not the right to do as I have only seen them in manuscript, they have not yet appeared in print.[1] These pieces are in a sense the thing itself — I shall have to fall back on description of the thing. The tirana, a dance common to the province of Andalusia, is accompanied by song. It has a decided rhythm, affording opportunities for grace and gesture, the women toying with their aprons, the men flourishing hats and handkerchiefs. The polo, or ole, is now a gipsy dance. Mr. Ellis asserts that it is a corruption of the sarabande! He goes on to say: "The so-called gipsy dances of Spain are Spanish dances which the Spaniards are tending to relinquish but which the gipsies have taken up with energy and skill." (This theory might be warmly contested.) The bolero, a comparatively modern dance, came to Spain through Italy. Mr. Philip Hale (Boston music critic /*Editor*) points out the fact that the bolero and the cachucha (which, by the way, one seldom hears of nowadays) were the popular Spanish dances when Mesdames Faviani and Dolores Tesrai, and their followers, Mlle. Noblet and Fanny Elssler, visited Paris. Fanny Elssler indeed is most frequently seen pictured in Spanish costume, and the cachucha was danced by her as often, I fancy, as Mme. Pavlowa dances *Le Cygne* of Saint-Saëns. Marie-Anne de Camargo, who acquired great fame as a dancer in France in the early eighteenth century, was born in Brussels but was of Spanish descent. She relied, however, on the Italian classic style for her success rather than on national Spanish dances. The seguidilla is a gipsy dance which has the same rhythm as the bolero but is more animated and stirring. Examples of these dances, and of the jota, fandango, and the sevillana, are to be met with in the compositions listed in the first section of this article (not included in this

149

volume / *Editor*), in the appendices of Soriano Fuertes's "History of Spanish Music," in Grove's Dictionary, in the numbers of "S.I.M." in which the letters of Emmanuel Chabrier occur, and in collections made by P. Lacome, published in Paris.

The jota is another dance in 3/4 time. Every province in Spain has its own jota, but the most famous variations are those of Aragon, Valencia, and Navarre. It is accompanied by the guitar, the *bandarria* (similar to the guitar), small drum, castanets and triangle. Mr. Hale says that its origin in the twelfth century is attributed to a Moor named Alben Jot who fled from Valencia to Aragon. "The jota," he continues, "is danced not only at merrymakings but at certain religious festivals and even in watching the dead. (Tomás Bretón writes me that he considers it ridiculous to attribute any such age (twelfth century) to the jota. His researches on the subject are embodied in a pamphlet (1911) entitled "Rápida ojeada histórica sobre la música española.") One called the 'Natividad del Señor' (Nativity of our Lord) is danced on Christmas eve in Aragon, and is accompanied by songs, and jotas are sung and danced at the crossroads, invoking the favour of the Virgin, when the festival of Our Lady del Pilar is celebrated at Saragossa."

Havelock Ellis's description of the jota is worth reproducing: "The Aragonaise jota, the most important and typical dance outside Andalusia, is danced by a man and a woman, and a kind of combat between them; most of the time they are facing each other, both using castanets and advancing and retreating in an apparently aggressive manner, the arms alternately slightly raised and lowered, and the legs, with a seeming attempt to trip the partner, kicking out alternately somewhat sidewise, as the body is rapidly supported first on one side and then on the other. It is a monotonous dance, with immense rapidity and vivacity in its monotony, but it has not the deliberate grace and fascination, the happy audacities of Andalusian dancing. There is, indeed, no faintest suggestion of voluptuousness in it, but it may rather be said, in the words of a modern poet, Salvador Rueda, to have in it 'the sound of helmets and plumes and lances and banners, the roaring of cannon, the neighing of horses, the shock of swords.'"

Chabrier, in his astounding and amusing letters from Spain, gives us vivid pictures and interesting information. This one, written to his friend, Edouard Moullé, from Granada, November 4, 1882, appeared in "S.I.M." April 15, 1911 (I have omitted the musical illustrations, which, however, possess great value for the student): "In a month I must leave adorable Spain. . . and say good-bye to the Spaniards — because, I say this only to you, they are very nice, the little girls! I have not seen a really ugly woman since I have been in Andalusia: I do not speak of the feet, they are so small that I have not seen them; the hands are tiny and well-kept and the arms of an exquisite contour; I speak only of what one can see, but they show a good deal; add the arabesques, the side-curls, and other ingenuities of the coiffure, the inevitable fan, the flower and the comb in the hair, placed well behind, the shawl of Chinese crêpe, with long fringe and embroidered in flowers, knotted around the figure, the arm bare, and the eye protected by eyelashes which are long enough to curl; the skin of dull white or orange colour, according to the race, all this smiling, gesticulating, dancing, drinking, and careless to the last degree. . .

"That is the Andalusian.

"Every evening we go with Alice to the café-concerts where the malagueñas, the Soledas, the Sapateados, and the Peterneras are sung; then the dances, absolutely Arab, to speak truth; if you can see them wriggle, unjoint their hips, contortion, I believe you would not try to get away! . . . At Malaga the dancing became so intense that I was compelled to take my wife away; it wasn't even amusing anymore. I can't write about it, but I remember it and I will describe it to you. I have no need to tell you that I have noted down many things; the tango, a kind of dance in which the women imitate the pitching of a ship (*le tangage du navire*) is the only dance in 2 time; all the others, all, are in

3/4 *(Seville)* or in 3/8 *(Malaga and Cadiz)*; — in the North it is different, there is some music in 5/8, very curious. The 2/4 of the tango is always like the habanera; this is the picture: one or two women dance, two silly men play it doesn't matter what on their guitars, and five or six women howl, with excruciating voices and in triplet figures impossible to note down because they change the air — every instant a new scrap of tune. They howl a series of figurations with syllables, words, rising voices, clapping hands which strike the six quavers, emphasizing the third and the sixth, cries of Anda! Anda! La Salud! eso es la Maraquita! gracia, nationidad! Baila, la chiquilla! Anda! Anda! Consuelo! Olé, la Lola, olé la Carmen! que gracia! que elegancia! all that to excite the young dancer. It is vertiginous — it is unspeakable!

"The Sevillana is another thing: it is in 3/4 time (and with castanets)... All this becomes extraordinarily alluring with two curls, a pair of castanets and a guitar. It is impossible to write down the malagueña. It is a melopoeia, however, which has a form and which always ends on the dominant, to which the guitar furnishes 3/8 time, and the spectator (when there is one) seated beside the guitarist, holds a cane between his legs and beats the syncopated rhythm; the dancers themselves instinctively syncopate the measures in a thousand ways, striking with their heels an unbelievable number of rhythms... It is all rhythm and dance: the airs scraped out by the guitarist have no value; besides, they cannot be heard on account of the cries of Anda! la chiquilla! que gracia! que elegancia! Anda! Olé! Olé! la chiquirritita! and the more the cries the more the dancer laughs with her mouth wide open, and turns her hips, and is mad with her body..."

Gautier thus describes this dance: "La *malagueña*, danse locale de Malaga, est vraiment d'une poésie charmante. Le cavalier parait d'abord, le *sombrero* sur les yeux, embossé dans sa cape écarlate comme un hidalgo qui se promène et cherche les aventures. La dame entre, drapée dans sa mantille, son éventail à la main, avec les façons d'une femme qui va faire un tour à l'Alameda. Le cavalier tâche de voir la figure de cette mystérieuse sirène; mais la coquette manoeuvre si bien de l'éventail, l'ouvre et le ferme si à propos, le tourne et le retourne si promptement à la hauteur de son joli visage, que le galant, désappointé, recule de quelques pas et s'avise d'un autre stratagème. Il fait parler des castagnettes sous son manteau. A ce bruit, la dame prête l'oreille; elle sourit, son sein palpite, la pointe de son petit pied de satin marque la mesure malgré elle; elle jette son éventail, sa mantille, et parait en folle toilette de danseuse, étincelante de paillette et de clinquants, une rose dans les cheveux, un grand peigne d'écaille sur le tête. Le cavalier se débarrasse de son masque et de sa cape, et tous deux exécutent un pas d'une originalité délicieuse." [2]

Curiously enough in a music critic's account of a voyage in Spain (H.T. Finck's "Spain and Morocco") only a single page is devoted to a discussion of Spanish music or dancing. The author is not sympathetic. The rhythmic and dynamic features of the performance which so aroused the delight of Chabrier only annoy Mr. Finck. I quote his account which begins with an experience at Murcia: "In the evening I came across an interesting performance in the street. A woman and a man were singing a duet, accompanying themselves with a guitar and a mandolin, making a peculiarly pleasing combination, infinitely superior to the performances of the Italian bards who accompany themselves with hand-organs or cheap harps, not to speak of the horrible German beer-bands which infest our streets. It was indeed so agreeable that I followed the couple for several blocks. But with the exception of a students' concert in Seville, it was almost the only good music I heard in Spain. Madrid and Barcelona have ambitious operatic performances in winter, and the Barcelonese go so far as to claim that they sing and understand Wagner better than the Berliners; but as the opera houses were closed while I was there, I have no comments to offer on this boast. In a café chantant which I visited in Seville I heard, instead of national airs, vulgar French women singing a French version of 'Champagne Charley' and similar vulgar things; no one, it is true, cared for these songs, whereas a rare bit of national melody in the program was wildly applauded; but fashion of course must have her sway. At another café the music was thoroughly Spanish, with guitar accompaniment; but, according to the usual Spanish custom, there were a dozen persons on the stage who clapped their hands so loudly, to mark the rhythm, that the music degenerated into a mere rhythmic noise accompanying the dancing. These dances interest the Spanish populace much more than any kind of music, and I was amused occasionally to see a group of working men looking on the grotesque amateur dancing of one or two of their number with an expression of supreme enjoyment, and clapping their hands in unison to keep time."

Seeing indifferent dancing performed, he affirms, by women who are no longer young, in the early part of his Spanish sojourn, Théophile Gautier, too, at first was inclined to treat Spanish dancing as a myth: "Les danses espagnoles n'existent qu'à Paris, comme les coquillages, qu'on ne trouve que chez les marchands de curiosités, et jamais sur le bord de la mer. O Fanny Elssler! qui êtes maintenant en Amérique chez les sauvages, même avant d'aller en Espagne, nous nous doutions bien que c'était vous qui aviez inventé la cachucha!"...[3] This was at Vitoria. In Madrid he writes: "On nous avait dit à Vitoria, à Burgos et à Valladolid, que les bonnes danseuses étaient à Madrid; à Madrid, l'on nous a dit que les véritables danseuses de cachucha n'existaient qu'en Andalousie, à Seville. Nous verrons bien; mais nous avons peur qu'en fait de danses espagnoles, il ne nous faille en revenir à Fanny Elssler et aux deux soeurs Noblet."...[4] In Andalusia he capitulated: "Les danseuses espagnoles, bien qu'elles n'aient pas le fini, la correction précise, l'élévation des danseuses françaises, leur sont, à mon avis, bien supérieures par la grâce et le charme; comme elles travaillent peu et ne s'assujetissent pas à ces terribles exercises d'assouplissement qui font ressembler une classe de danse à une salle de torture, elles évitent cette maigreur de cheval entrainé qui donne à nos ballets quelque chose de trop macabre et de trop anatomique; elles conservent les contours et les rondeurs de leur sexe; elles ont l'air de femmes qui dansent et non pas de danseures, ce qui est bien différent... En Espagne les pieds quittent à peine la terre; point de ces grands ronds de jambe, de ces écarts qui font ressembler une femme à un compas forcé, et qu'on trouve là-bas d'une indécence révoltante. C'est le corps qui danse, ce sont les reins qui se cambrent, les flancs qui ploient, la taille qui se tord avec une souplesse d'almée ou de couleuvre. Dans les poses renversées, les epaules de la danseuse vont presque toucher la terre; les bras, pâmés et morts, ont une flexibilité, une mollesse d'écharpe dénouée; on dirait que les mains peuvent à peine soulever et faire babiller les castagnettes d'ivoire aux cordons tressés d'or; et cependant, au moment venu, des bonds de jeune jaguar succèdent à cette langueur voluptueuse, et prouvent que ces corps, doux comme la soie, enveloppent des muscles d'acier...[5]

As it is on these dances that composers invariably base their Spanish music (not alone Albéniz, Chapí, Bretón, and Granados, but Chabrier, Ravel, Laparra, and Bizet, as well) we may linger somewhat longer on their delights. The following compelling description is from Richard Ford's highly readable "Gatherings from Spain": "The dance which is closely analogous to the *Ghowasee* of the Egyptians, and the *Nautch* of the Hindoos, is called the *Ole* by Spaniards, the *Romalis* by their gipsies; the soul and essence of it consists in the expression of a certain sentiment, one not indeed of a very sentimental or correct character. The ladies, who seem to have no bones, resolve the problem of perpetual motion, their feet having comparatively a sinecure, as the whole person performs a pantomime, and trembles like as aspen leaf; the flexible form and Terpsichore figure of a young Andalusian girl — be she gipsy or not — is said, by the learned, to have been designed by nature as the fit frame for her voluptuous imagination.

"Be that as it may, the scholar and classical commentator will every moment quote Martial, etc., when he beholds the unchanged balancing of hands, raised as if to catch showers of roses, the tapping of the feet, and the serpentine quivering movements. A contagious excitement seizes the spectators, who, like Orientals, beat time with their hands in measured cadence, and at every pause applaud with cries and clappings. The damsels, thus encouraged, continue in violent action until nature is all but exhausted; then aniseed brandy, wine, and *alpisteras* are handed about, and the fête, carried on to early dawn, often concludes in broken heads, which here are called 'gipsy's fare.' These dances appear, to a stranger from the chilly north, to be more marked by energy than by grace, nor have the legs less to do than the body, hips, and arms. The sight of this unchanged pastime of antiquity, which excites the Spaniard to frenzy, rather disgusts an English spectator, possibly from some national malorganization, for, as Molière says, 'l'Angle-terre a produit des grands hommes dans les sciences et les beaux arts, mais pas un grand danseur — allez lire l'histoire.' "[6] (A fact as true in our day as it was in Molière's.)[7]

Arthur Symons has written a very beautiful passage to describe a gipsy dancing. If you have seen Doloretes you may think of her while you read it: "All Spanish dancing, and especially the dancing of the gipsies, in which it is seen in its most characteristic development, has a sexual origin, and expresses, as Eastern dancing does, but less crudely, the pantomime of physical love. In the typical gipsy dance as I saw it danced by a beautiful Gitana at Seville, there is something of mere gaminerie and something of the devil; the automatic tramp-tramp of the children and the lascivious pantomime of a very learned art of love. Thus it has all the excitement of something spontaneous and studied, of vice and a kind of naughty innocence, of the thoughtless gaiety of youth as well as the knowing humour of experience. For it is a dance full of humour, fuller of humour than of passion; passion indeed it mimics on the purely animal side, and with a sort of coldness even in its frenzy. It is capable of infinite variations; it is a drama, but a drama improvised on a given theme; and it might go on indefinitely, for it is conditioned only by the pantomime which we know to have wide limits. A motion more or less and it becomes obscene or innocent; it is always on a doubtful verge, and thus gains its extraordinary fascination. I held my breath as I watched the gipsy in the Seville dancing-hall; I felt myself swaying unconsciously to the rhythm of her body, of her beckoning hands, of the glittering smile that came and went in her eyes. I seemed to be drawn into a shining whirlpool, in which I turned, turned, hearing the buzz of water settling over my head. The guitar buzzed, buzzed, in a prancing rhythm, the gipsy coiled about the floor, in her trailing dress, never so much as showing her ankles, with a rapidity concentrated upon itself; her hands beckoned, reached out, clutched delicately, lived to their finger-tips; her body straightened, bent, the knees bent and straightened, the heels beat on the floor, carrying her backwards and round; the toes pointed, paused, pointed, and the body drooped or rose into immobility, a smiling, significant pause of the whole body. Then the motion became again more vivid, more restrained, as if teased by some unseen limits, as if turning upon itself in the vain desire of escape, as if caught in its own toils; more feverish, more fatal, the humour turning painful, with the pain of achieved desire; more earnest, more eager, with the languor in which desire dies triumphant."

On certain days the sevillana is danced before the high altar of the cathedral at Seville. The Reverend Henry Cart de Lafontaine ("Proceedings of the Musical Association"; London, thirty-third session, 1906-7) gives the following account of it, quoting a "French author": While Louis XIII was reigning over France, the Pope heard much talk of the Spanish dance called the 'Sevillana.' He wished to satisfy himself, by actual eye-witness, as to the character of this dance, and expressed his wish to a bishop of the diocese of Seville, who every year visited Rome. Evil tongues made the bishop responsible for the primary suggestion of the idea. Be that as it may, the bishop, on his return to Seville, had twelve youths well instructed in all the intricate measures of this Andalusian dance. He had to choose youths, for how could he present maidens to the horrified glance of the Holy Father? When his little troop was thoroughly schooled and perfected, he took the party to Rome, and the audience was arranged. The 'Sevillana' was danced in one of the rooms of the Vatican. The Pope warmly complimented the young executants, who were dressed in beautiful silk costumes of the period. The bishop humbly asked for permission to perform this dance at certain fêtes in the cathedral church at Seville, and further pleaded for a restriction of this privilege to that church alone. The Pope, hoist by his own petard, did not like to refuse, but granted the privilege with this restriction, that it should only last so long as the costumes of the dancers were wearable. Needless to say, these costumes are, therefore, objects of constant repair, but they are supposed to retain their identity even to this day. And this is the reason why the twelve boys who dance the 'Sevillana' before the high altar in the cathedral on certain feast days are dressed in the costume belonging to the reign of Louis XIII."

This is a very pretty story, but it is not uncontradicted . . . Has any statement been made about Spanish dancing or music which has been allowed to go uncontradicted? Look upon that picture and upon this: "As far as it is possible to ascertain from records," says Rhoda G. Edwards in the "Musical Standard," "this dance would seem always to have been in use in Seville cathedral; when the town was taken from the Moors in the thirteenth century it was undoubtedly an established custom and in 1428 we find the six boys recognized as an integral part of the chapter by Pope Eugenius IV. The dance is known as the *(sic)* 'Los Scises,' or dance of the six boys who, with four others, dance it before the high altar at Benediction on the three evenings before Lent and in the octaves of Corpus Christi and La Purissima (the conception of Our Lady). The dress of the boys is most picturesque, page costumes of the time of Philip III being worn, blue for La Purissima and red satin doublets slashed with blue for the other occasion; white hats with blue and white feathers are also worn whilst dancing. The dance is usually of twenty-five minutes' duration and in form seems quite unique, not resembling any of the other Spanish dance-forms, or in fact those of any other country. The boys accompany the symphony on castanets and sing a hymn in two parts whilst dancing."

Another account of this dance in the cathedral may be found in deAmicis's "Spain and the Spaniards." ... H.T. Finck saw this dance and he devotes a short paragraph to it on p.56 of his "Spain and Morocco." Arthur Symons's description in his essay on "Seville" in "Cities" is charming enough to quote: "There was but little light except about the altar, which blazed with candles; suddenly a curtain was drawn aside, and the sixteen boys, in their blue and white costume, holding plumed hats in their hands, came forward and knelt before the altar. The priests, who had been chanting, came up from the choir; the boys rose, and formed in two eights, facing each other, in front of the altar, and the priests knelt in a semi-circle around them. Then an unseen orchestra began to play, and the boys put on their hats, and began to sing the *coplas* in honour of the Virgin:

'O mi, O mi amada
Immaculada!'

as they sang to a dance measure. After they had sung the *coplas* they began to dance, still singing. It was a kind of solemn minuet, the feet never taken from the ground, a minuet of delicate stepping and intricate movement, in which a central square would form, divide, a whole line passing through the opposite line, the outer ends then repeating one another's movements while the others turned and divided again in the middle. The first movement was very slow, the second faster, ending with a pirouette; then came two movements without singing, but with the accompaniment of castanets, the first movement again very slow, the second a quick rattle of the castanets, like the rattling of kettle-drums, but done without raising the hands above the level of the elbows. Then the whole thing was repeated from the beginning, the boys flourished off their hats, dropped on their knees before the altar, and went quickly out. One or two verses were chanted, the Archbishop gave his benediction, and the ceremony was over.

"And, yes, I found it perfectly dignified, perfectly religious, without a suspicion of levity or indecorum. This consecration of the dance, this turning of a posssible vice into a means of devotion, this bringing of the people's art, the people's passion, which in Seville is dancing, into the church, finding it a place there, is precisely one of those acts of divine worldly wisdom which the Church has so often practised in her conquest of the world."[8]

From another author we learn that religious dancing is to be seen elsewhere in Spain than at Seville cathedral. At one time, it is said to have been common. The pilgrims to the shrine of the Virgin at Montserrat were wont to dance, and dancing took place in the churches of Valencia, Toledo, and Jerez. Religious dancing continued to be common, especially in Catalonia up to the seventeenth century. An account of the dance in the Seville cathedral may be found in "Los Españoles Pintados por si Mismos" (pages 287-91).

This very incomplete and rambling record of Spanish dancing should include some mention of the fandango. The origin of the word is obscure, but the dance is obviously one of the gayest and wildest of the Spanish dances. Like the malagueña it is in 3/8 time, but it is quite different in spirit from that sensuous form of terpsichorean enjoyment. La Argentina informs me that "fandango" in Spanish suggests very much what "bachanale" does in English or French. It is a very old dance, and may be a survival of a Moorish dance, as Desrat suggests. Mr. Philip Hale found the following account of it:

"Like an electric shock, the notes of the fandango animate all hearts. Men and women, young and old, acknowledge the power of this air over the ears and soul of every Spaniard. The young men spring to their places, rattling castanets, or imitating their sound by snapping their fingers. The girls are remarkable for the willowy languor and lightness of their movements, the voluptuousness of their attitudes — beating the exactest time with tapping heels. Partners tease and entreat and pursue each other by turns. Suddenly the music stops, and each dancer shows his skill by remaining absolutely motionless, bounding again in the full life of the fandango as the orchestra strikes up. The sound of the guitar, the violin, the rapid tic-tac of heels (*taconeos*), the crack of fingers and castanets, the supple swaying of the dancers, fill the spectators with ecstasy.

"The music whirls along in a rapid triple time. Spangles glitter; the sharp clank of ivory and ebony castanets beats out the cadence of strange, throbbing, deafening notes — assonances unknown to music, but curiously characteristic, effective, and intoxicating. Amidst the rustle of silks, smiles gleam over white teeth, dark eyes sparkle and droop, and flash up again in flame. All is flutter and glitter, grace and animation — quivering, sonorous, passionate, seductive. *Olé! Olé!* Faces beam and burn. *Olé! Olé!*

"The bolero intoxicates, the fandango inflames."

Mr. Philip Hale's account of the fandango . . . is from the . . . anonymous, incomplete, and somewhat incorrect translation of Gaston Vuillier's "La Danse" (Hachette et Cie, 1898). In the original work this description of the fandango seems to be attributed to Tomás de Iriarte although the text is a little ambiguous. In the English translation called, "A History of Dancing," Chapter VIII is mainly devoted to Spanish dancing; in the original work it is Chapter IX. Vuillier derived most of his material from the Baron Charles Davillier's elaborate work, "l'Espagne," which is illustrated by Gustave Doré. Vuillier quotes Davillier very freely. Davillier's chapters on Spanish dancing (Chapters XIV and XV) are extremely interesting and much of their material the Baron gathered himself. There is for example a description of La Campanera dancing to the indifferent music provided by a blind violinist whose tunes prove so uninspiring that Doré seizes the violin from his trembling old fingers and plays it himself with great effect. Davillier describes Doré as a violinist of the first order who had won praise from Rossini. On another occasion Davillier and Doré, stimulated by the dancing of gipsies, enter into the sport themselves, wildly tap their heels, wave their arms, and circle with the gitanas while a large group applauds. This book which was published by Hachette in Paris in 1874 was brought out in New York, in J. Thomson's translation, with the original illustrations, by Scribner, Welford, and Armstrong in 1876. In the American edition the two French chapters are rolled into one, Chapter XIV.

I found the following reference to the fandango in Philip Thicknesse's remarkably interesting and exceedingly curious book, "A Year's Journey through France and Part of Spain" (London; 1777): "In no part of the world, therefore, are women more caressed and attended to, than in Spain. Their deportment in public is grave and modest; yet they are very much addicted to pleasure; nor is there scarce one among them that cannot, nay that will not dance the *Fandango* in private, either in the decent or the indecent manner. I have seen it danced both ways, by a pretty woman, than which nothing can be more *immodestly agreeable*; and I was shewn a young lady at *Barcelona* who in the midst of this dance ran out of the room, telling her partner she could *stand* it no longer; — he ran after her, to be sure, and must be answerable for the consequences. I find in the music of the *Fandango,* written under one bar, *Salido,* which signifies *going out;* it is where the woman is to part a little from her partner, and to move slowly by herself; and I suppose it was at *that bar* the lady was so overcome, as to determine her not to return. The words *Perra Salida* should therefore be played at that bar, when the ladies dance it in the high *goût*."

Philip Thicknesse is one of the undeservedly forgotten figures of the eighteenth century. He wrote twenty-four books, including the first Life of Thomas Gainsborough, whom he claims to have discovered and which contains accounts of pictures which have disappeared, "A Treatise on the Art of Decyphering and of Writing in Cypher with an Harmonic Alphabet," and the aforementioned account of a journey through France and Spain which contains one of the earliest sympathetic descriptions of Montserrat. Thicknesse led far from a dull life and its course was marked by a series of violent quarrels. Born in 1719 he was in Georgia with General Oglethorpe in 1735. Later he fought wild negroes in Jamaica and cruised in the Mediterranean with Admiral Medley. In 1762 he had a dispute with Francis Vernon (afterwards Lord Orwell and Earl of Shipbrooke) then Colonel of the Suffolk militia; and having sent the Colonel the ridiculous present of a wooden gun became involved in an action for libel with the result that he was confined three months in the King's Bench Prison and fined £300. He was married three times. For his son, by his second marriage, Baron Audley, he conceived a deep hatred of which there is an echo in his will wherein he desires his right hand to be cut off and sent to Lord Audley to remind him of his duty to God after having so long abandoned the duty he owed to his father. The title of his last book also bears witness to this feud: "Memoirs and Anecdotes of Philip Thicknesse, late Lieutenant Governor of Land Guard Fort and unfortunately father to George Touchet, Baron Audley." In 1774 his twenty year friendship with Gainsborough ended in a wretched squabble. In 1775 a decree of chancery ratified by the House of Lords, to which he appealed, deprived him of what he considered his right to £12,000 from the family of his first wife. Feeling himself driven out of his country, accompanied by his third wife, two children and a monkey, he went to live in

Spain, but he was back in England in a year and published the book from which I have quoted. His third wife, Anne Ford, was celebrated as a musician and you may find some account of her in the old Grove's Dictionary. She played the guitar, the viola de gamba, and the "musical glasses" and sang airs by Handel and the early Italians. The customs inspector at Cette on the way to Spain found "a bass viol, two guittars, a fiddle, and some other musical instruments" in Thicknesse's baggage. Thicknesse died in 1792 and was buried in the Protestant Cemetary in Boulogne. The greater part of his work in Spain is devoted to an account of Montserrat, which he visited before its despoliation.

It can be well understood that the study of Spanish dancing and its music must be carried on in Spain. Mr. Ellis tells us why: "Another characteristic of Spanish dancing, and especially of the most typical kind called flamenco, lies in its accompaniments, and particularly in the fact that under proper conditions all the spectators are themselves performers. . .Thus it is that at the end of a dance an absolute silence often falls, with no sound of applause: the relation of performers and public has ceased to exist. . . .The finest Spanish dancing is at once killed or degraded by the presence of an indifferent or unsympathetic public, and that is probably why it cannot be transplanted, but remains local." [9]

(James Huneker's Spanish experiences as related in the chapter on Madrid in "The New Cosmopolis," New York, 1915, seem to have been unfortunate. There are those who would disagree with every separate statement in the following paragraph: "The best Spanish dancing is not to be found in Spain today. You must go to Paris for Otero and Carmencita. Nor is the most characteristic cookery in Spain; at least not in Madrid. The greatest Spanish opera was composed by the Frenchman Bizet.")

"At the end of a dance an absolute silence often falls". . . I am again in an underground café in Amsterdam. It is the eve of the Queen's birthday, and the Dutch are celebrating. The low, smoke-wreathed room is crowded with students, soldiers, and women. Now a weazened female takes her place at the piano, on a slightly raised platform at one side of the room. She begins to play. The dancing begins. It is not woman with man; the dancing is informal. Some dance together, and some dance alone; some sing the melody of the tune, others shriek, but all make a noise. Faster and faster and louder and louder the music is pounded out, and the dancing becomes wilder and wilder. A tray of glasses is kicked from the upturned palm of a sweaty waiter. Waiter, broken glass, dancer, all lie, a laughing heap, on the floor. A soldier and a woman stand in opposite corners, facing the corners; when without turning, they back towards the middle of the room at a furious pace; the collision is appalling. Hand in hand the mad dancers encircle the room, throwing confetti, beer, anything. A heavy stein crushes two teeth — the wound bleeds — but the dancer does not stop. Noise and action and colour all become synonymous. There is no escape from the force. I am dragged into the circle. Suddenly the music stops. All the dancers stop. The soldier no longer looks at the woman by his side; not a word is spoken. People lumber toward chairs. The woman looks for a glass of water to assuage the pain of her bleeding mouth. I think Jaques-Dalcroze is right when he seeks to unite spectator and actor, drama and public.

In the preceding section I may have too strongly insisted upon the relation of the folk-song to the dance. It is true that the two are seldom separated in performance (although not all songs are danced; for example, the *cañas* and *playeras* of Andalusia). However, most of the folk-songs of Spain are intended to be danced; they are built on dance-rhythms and they bear the names of dances. Thus the jota is always danced to the same music, although the variations are great at different times and in different provinces. It is, of course, when the folk-songs are danced that they make their best effect, in the polyrhythm achieved by

the opposing rhythms of guitar-player, dancer, and singer. When there is no dancer the defect is sometimes overcome by some one tapping a stick on the ground in imitation of resounding heels.
(*March 20, 1916*)

— From *The Music of Spain,* Knopf, 1918.

1. It is not possible to be sure at this later time to which poems by Gertrude Stein Van Vechten refers; it is likely they are among the ones published after her death by Yale University Press, edited by Van Vechten. In the volume, *Bee Time Vine,* (published in 1953) some of the poems were composed in Spain, c. 1913-15. The subject in the title poem, "Bee Time Vine," is Spain and begins: "Bee time vine be vine truth devine truth. Be vine be vine be vine truth, be vine be vine be vine."
    When read aloud, the rhythm is there. / *Editor*
2. (translation) The malaguena, the local dance of Malaga, is really a charming poem. The cavalier appears first, hat over his eyes, wrapped in his scarlet cape like a nobleman who is prowling around, looking for adventures. The lady appears, draped in her mantilla, her fan in her hand, with the look of a lady who is going to take a walk on the Alameda.
    The cavalier tries to see the face of this mysterious siren, but the coquette uses her fan so well, opens it and closes it, so skillfully that the cavalier, disappointed, retreats several steps, and thinks of another stratagem. Under his cloak he makes the castanets speak. At this noise, the lady lends an ear; she smiles, her breast palpitates, the point of her little satin-covered foot taps out the rhythm in spite of herself; she throws aside the fan, her mantilla, and appears in the wild costume of a dancer — glittering spangles and tinsel, a rose in her hair, a large tortoise-shell comb on her head. The cavalier casts aside his mask and cape and both the cavalier and the lady execute a dance of delightful originality.
3. (translation) Spanish dances exist only in Paris, like the shells which one finds in the curio shops and never at the seashore. O Fanny Elssler! You who are now in America among the savages; even before going to Spain, we really suspected that it was you who had invented the cachucha.
4. (translation) They had told us in Vitoria, in Burgos, and in Valladolid that the good dancers were in Madrid; in Madrid they told us

that the real dancers of the cachucha existed only in Andalucia, in Seville. We shall see; but we are afraid that for the Spanish dance, we must return to Fanny Elssler and the Noblet sisters.
5. (translation) Spanish dancers, although they may not have the perfection, the precise correctness, the loftiness of the French dancers, are quite superior to them, in my opinion, in charm and grace, since they work little and do not subject themselves to those terrible limbering-up exercises which make a dancing class resemble a torture room; they avoid that leaness of the trained horse which gives to our ballets something too macabre and too anatomical; they retain the contours and roundness of their sex; they look like women who dance and not like dancers, which is quite different.

In Spain, the feet hardly leave the ground; none of those *ronds de jambe,* those *écarts* which make a woman look like a shaken compass, and one finds therein a revolting indecency. It is the body which dances, the back which is arched, the sides which bend, the waist which twists with the suppleness of an *almeh* (Egyptian dancing girl) or a snake. In the *poses renversées,* the shoulders of the dancers almost touch the ground, the arms, limp and dead, have the flexibility, the softness of an untied scarf; one might say that the hands can hardly raise and click the ivory castanets with their cords of golden braids; and however, when the moment arrives, the leaps of a young jaguar follow this voluptuous languor and prove that these bodies, soft as silk, envelop muscles of steel.
6. (translation) England has produced some great men in science and the fine arts, but no one great dancer — go read history.
7. Van Vechten was agreeing with Moliére in 1916 that England had produced no great dancers. He would have had to revise his opinion by the mid century when he wrote on Alicia Markova. / *Editor*
8. A modern day counterpart of secular music in the church can be found in the jazz concerts and rock festivals now included in the repertoire of many churches in America. / *Editor*
9. All Havelock Ellis quotes are from *The Soul of Spain,* 1909. / *Editor*

5

Léo Delibes

"Delibes is the father of the modern ballet."

Léo Delibes

I am tired of the "Six." I am weary of Erik Satie. I am fed up with Malipiero. The music of Zoltan Kodaly has begun to pall on me. I have consigned my Arnold Schönberg scores to the flames and tossed Alfredo Casella into the dust-bin. I have presented such examples of the genius of Poulenc as I possessed to my grocer's daughter and my erstwhile copy of Lord Berner's *Three Little Funeral Marches* is now the property of the policeman on the corner. I am gorged with Ornstein and Prokofieff. DeFalla and Stravinsky are anathema to me. Béla Bartók is a neo-zany. I am sick of Greek tunics and bare legs, satiated with oriental dancing, Persian, Javanese, Chinese, and Polovtsian, surfeited with turkey trots and bunny hugs and fox trots, bored with tangos and maxixes, boleros and seguidillas, Argentine and Spanish dances of whatever nature. I have had my fill of ballroom dancing, cakewalks, pigeon-wings, clogs, jazz, and hoe-downs. Terpsichore has been such a favorite of late, literary, pictorial, musical, and even social, that the muse has become inflatedly self-conscious, afflicted with a bad case of megalomania. Personally, I wave her away. There is, of course, a reason for this reaction, a stimulant for this new litany: in cleaning out an old music cabinet today I stumbled upon the score of *Coppélia:*[1] the distinguished, spirited, singing, luminous, melodies of Delibes rang again in my ears, the eyes of memory focused on the fluffed tarlatan skirt, the suggestive fleshings terminating in the pointed toe, and, quite suddenly, all "modern" music and dancing assumed the quality of fustian.

"Every dance recalls love. Every ballet leaves us sighing with regret," writes André Suarès. "This mad Maenad becomes intoxicated in her own fashion; she burns only with the wine she drinks; she does not aspire to an internal intoxication, that which the vine of the heart opens to the spirit. She has no subjectivity; she is not meditative; she is wholly carnal and voluptuous; she is not even melancholy, her nature is light. Thus, having humbly grasped the hand of music, held music in her arms, the dance betrays music. She asks music for his great heart passionate and tender, of which she makes nothing. She does not even offer music her own heart in return because she has no heart to offer. Like youth, she can only bestow élan and caprice. What is she then, for art and the supreme desire of man, but the most charming body, even if she be bereft of soul?"

The classic costume, the tutu, serves to accentuate this fantastic, carnal quality of the ballet. What fascinations of the imagination it immediately evokes, metamorphosing the dancer into a dragon-fly, a great moth, or a flower swaying in the wind, suggestive of nymphs and Banshees and faraway, faded, immortal things! The fluffy tarlatan and the tight bodice emphasize the wasp-waist, the frailty of the arms and legs. Sex is both concealed and awakened. The pointed toe gives the illusion to this mythological creature of an airy defiance of the laws of gravity. She becomes, indeed, a brilliant insect, hovering between heaven and earth. "The ballet," wrote Théophile Gautier in a happy phrase, "is music that one can see." See in a dream, he might have added, for surely there is a sense of unreality about this art, created artificially and consciously by its devotees, which makes it, thanks to its very conventions and limitations, something rich and strange.

Turning the leaves of this crepuscular score, I recall the names of dancers, some of them born and dead before Delibes's day: Maria Taglioni, the glamorous, Fanny Elssler, the saucy, Fanny Cerito, Carlotta Grisi, beloved of Gautier, Rita Sangalli, and Rosita Mauri, who forswore caviar because the Tsar, at one of her representations, turned his gaze from the stage to converse with his companions. What pictures of pleasant periods are brought before the eye of the mind by the very names of these ladies! And the names of these ladies and other lulling reveries have been awakened in me by a glimpse of a tattered score by Léo Delibes.

The significance of Delibes, albeit he himself assuredly owed something to Auber and Offenbach, in the history of French music is not, perhaps, generally recognized. More frequently, probably, it is entirely ignored. It was an agreeable experience, therefore, to discover a review by Emile Vuillermoz, appropos of a recent Parisian revival of *Le roi l'a dit,* in which the statement is made: "Such works as *Le roi l'a dit* and *Lakmé* have a considerable importance in our musical history. Delibes is the great forerunner of the 'artist-writer' from which our modern school has evolved. It is he who has given to our musicians the taste to dispose the notes of a chord, the timbre of an orchestration, the voices of an ensemble, with an attentive ingenuity which multiplies discoveries with each measure. His influence, and that of Edouard Lalo, have been decisive on the musicians of our time."

Another debt which music owes to Delibes is not owed exclusively by France; it is an international obligation. Before he began to compose his ballets, music for dancing, for the most part, consisted of tinkle-tinkle melodies with marked rhythm. Dancing in France, and often elsewhere (I am speaking, naturally, only of the ballet) was not deeply expressive in its nature. Its spectators were satisified with technical feats of virtuosity. Dancers were compared on their respective abilities to execute the *entrechat* and the *pirouette.* Taglioni and Elssler, to be sure, transcended the technical limitations of their art, evolving an imaginative and spirituelle contribution to the dance fully appreciated in early nineteenth century literature. They accomplished this through their own personalities, aided by the traditional, mystic costume, the garb of their priesthood, which endowed their movements with an element of fantasy. They received meager assistance from the music to which they danced. For these sublime rites, the simplest and most banal tunes, the baldest rhythm, the most threadbare harmony, sufficed. Nay more, music with any true verve or character was repudiated as actually likely to exercise a detrimental effect. It was Delibes who revolutionized this puerile ideal of ballet music, introducing in his scores a symphonic element, a wealth of graceful melody, and a richness of harmonic fibre, based, it is safe to hazard, on a healthy distaste for routine. *Coppélia* and *Sylvia*, then, are the forerunners of such elaborate contemporary scores as Tcherepnine's *Narcisse*, Debussy's *Jeux*, Ravel's *Daphnis et Chloë*, Strauss's *The Legend of Joseph*, and Stravinsky's *Petrouchka*. Beyond any manner of doubt, Delibes is the father of the modern ballet.

II

Clément-Philibert-Léo Delibes was born on February 21, 1836 at Saint-Germain-du-Val, a village situated in the Sarthe, near La Flèche. The death of his father having left the family without resources, his mother took him to Paris in 1848. He was admitted to the Conservatory, and at his first contest he won the second prize for solfège; the following year (1850), he won the first prize. During this period he was choir boy at the Madeleine. He studied pianoforte with Le Coupey, organ with Benoist, harmony with Bazin, and advanced composition with Adolphe Adam. In 1853, the latter exerted his influence to secure for his pupil a position as répétiteur at the Théâtre-Lyrique. He also became organist at St. Pierre de Chaillot and elsewhere before his appointment at St.-Jean-St.-François, where he was organist from 1862 to 1871. This appears to have been a traditional occupation with French composers. César Franck, Charles-Marie Widor, and Camille Saint-Saëns were all organists in Paris churches.

Very early in his career, Delibes began to write for the theatre, modestly at first, operettas and opéras-bouffes, which have been forgotten. His first effort appears to have been a piece in one act, *Deux sous de charbon,* produced at the Folies-Nouvelles in 1855. He wrote other operettas for the Kursaal d'Ems, the Bouffes-Parisiens, the Variétés, and the Athénée: *Les deux vieilles gardes* (1856); *l'Omelette a la Follembûche* (1859); *Le serpent à plumes* (1864); *l'Ecossais de*

Chatou (1869); etc. Two of his one-act light operas, *Monsieur Griffard* (1857) and *Le jardinier el son seigneur* (1863), were written for and produced at the Théâtre-Lyrique. He also composed several choruses and a mass. In 1863, he was engaged as répétiteur at the Opéra, and, in 1865, second chorus-master, under Victor Massé. In 1865, his cantata, *Alger*, was performed.

Having been commissioned to compose a ballet, *La Source* (performed for the first time, November 12, 1866), in collaboration with Minkus, the Polish musician, his share of the score (the second and third scenes, in this ballet in four scenes, are the work of Delibes) proved so melodious and so much more distinguished and original than that of his confrère, that Minkus found himself completely eclipsed. Delibes was next asked to write an interpolation, *Le pas des fleurs,* for a revival of Adolphe Adam's ballet, *Le Corsaire,* on October 21, 1867. His masterpiece, *Coppélia,* was produced May 25, 1870. His principal songs were published in 1872, the year of his marriage to a daughter of Mme. Denain, an actress of the Comédie Française. These included the celebrated *Les filles de Cadiz* and *Bonjour Suzon* (on poems by Alfred de Musset), *Avril* (Rémy Belleau), and *Myrto* (Armand Silvestre). *Le roi l'a dit* was produced at the Opéra-Comique, May 24, 1873, and *Sylvia,* at the Opéra, June 14, 1876. *La mort d'Orphée,* a "grand scena," was performed at the Trocadéro concerts in 1878; *Jean de Nivelle,* at the Opéra-Comique, March 8, 1880, and *Lakmé,* at the Opéra-Comique, April 14, 1883. He wrote incidental music for a revival of *Le roi s'amuse* at the Comédie-Française, November 22, 1882, and a five-act opera, *Kassya,* on which Massenet put the finishing touches, including the composition of the recitatives, after the composer's death, was performed at the Opéra-Comique, March 21, 1893. For a time, under the name of Eloi Delibès, he contributed musical criticism to the *Gaulois.*

In 1877, Delibes was made a Chevalier of the Legion of Honour. In January, 1881, he succeeded Henri Reber, recently deceased, as professor of advanced composition at the Conservatory. In December, 1884, he was elected a member of the Institut, succeeding Victor Massé, and in 1889, he was promoted to the grade of officer of the Legion of Honour. He died in Paris, January 16, 1891, and a memoir by E. Guiraud was published in 1892.

III

His operas, constructed according to a formula that was once fashionable, are a little tarnished. *Lakmé,* awakening bizarrely confused memories of Marie Van Zandt, Bessie Abott, Luisa Tetrazzini, and Maria Barrientos, retains some of its vitality and still remains in the repertory of the Paris Opéra-Comique (and of the Metropolitan Opera House!). Occasionally, this lyric perversion of "Le mariage de Loti" is given elsewhere so that some florid soprano may warble *The Bell-Song.* Pauline L'Allemand was the first New York Lakmé; Adelina Patti, the second. The score has the monotony and the clotting languor of the East. After the first act, all souls who are sensitive to suggestion are likely to fall asleep. *Le roi l'a dit* is interesting in its historical aspects; I have already quoted M. Vuillermoz in this regard. I heard *Jean de Nivelle* at the Gaieté-Lyrique at Paris fourteen or fifteen years ago when Arlette was sung by Nicot-Bilbaut-Vauchelet, the daughter of the soprano who created this florid rôle in 1880. This Louis XI lyric drama is Delibes's contribution to Tannhäuserism. Russia, Germany, France, all suffered from this quaint disease.

Saint-Saëns once remarked with contemptuous bitterness: "French criticism has not reproached Delibes for not being a melodist; he has made some operettas." The gift of melody, however, is rare and it is a gift the gods bestowed on Delibes to the partial exclusion of Saint-Saëns. It is not in his operas that this gift may be studied most advantageously, although neither *The Bell-Song* nor the *Barcarolle* in *Lakmé* is to be scoffed at. The best pages in the score, however, are those devoted to the ballet, the exotic *Terâna,* the *Rektah,* and the Persian dance (music employed by Ruth St. Denis in her creation of *Radha*), and it is in his music for the ballet generally that Delibes excelled and in which, as has been intimated already, he made certain innovations. Ballet music, heretofore, had been subservient to the dancers, and it was believed, it would seem, that banality was essential to its success. Delibes's ballet music is piquant and pictureque, nervous and brilliant, shot with color and curious instrumental effects, subtle in rhythm; above all, his melody has a highly distinguished line and the texture is symphonic.

Sylvia, ou la nymphe de Diane, created by Rita Sangalli (who ten years later became the Baronne de St.-Pierre) at the Paris Opéra, June 14, 1876, is an evocation today (it has recently been revived) of a period; it is Second Empire classicism, if you like, but the music remains as *pimpant,* as exhilaratingly fresh as ever. A happy fragrance, a delightfully artificial, if somewhat heartless, charm hovers over this score. Delibes, aware of his limitations, or governed purely by his taste, deliberately excluded the barbaric and the savage from his work. *Les chasseresses,* the *Valse lente,* the *Cortège de Bacchus,* all retain their peculiar seductions, and the pizzicati divertissement of the slave has achieved a world-fame.

Coppélia, ou la fille aux yeux d'email, is assuredly his masterpiece. From the *Prélude* and the *Valse lente,* to which the adorable Swanilda[2] floats across the scene almost as soon as the curtains part, through the Csárdás, the Mazurka, on to the end of the work, it is a model of concise and witty music, spirited and delicate melody. There are, to be sure, sentimental passages, but on the whole, Delibes is less sentimental than Gounod. His tunes usually move at a brisk pace. They have all the lustre of a polka by Offenbach, and something more in the way of glamour. Perusing this old score, I dream again of the languorous delights of the ballet, the real ballet and, for the moment, I am no modern. It has even occurred to me to wonder if any com-

poser gifted with the power to create melody has ever found it necessary to try to create anything else.
(*May 9, 1922*)

— From *Excavations*, Knopf, 1926.

1. *Coppélia* celebrated its 100th birthday in 1970. Walter Terry in *The Saturday Review* of June 6, 1970, gives a detailed account of the ballet's history during the century since its Paris premiere. / *Editor*
2. See review of Pavlova's interpretation of Swanilda which she danced for her American debut on March 1, 1910. / *Editor*

Index

The liberal number of names and titles in this collection dictates that a subjective selection of the important ones be indexed. When several works by a single composer are indicated, they are listed with the author. Popular titles in the text, ie., *Carnaval, Narcisse, Prince Igor,* are indexed by title. Compositions known by more than one title are cross-referenced. / *Editor*

Adam, Adolphe, 174
   Giselle, 46, 99-100, 103, 104, 123-124, 126, 127, 130
Aguglia, Mimi, 136, 141 (footnote)
Ailey, Alvin, 42-45
Aldrich, Richard, xiii, 6
Allan, Maud, xiii, 7, 15, 29-32
Alonso, Alicia, 46
Altschuler, Modest, 30, 32
Arensberg, Walter Conrad, 68
Argentina, La, 137, 138-139, 142-143, 160
Ashton, Frederick, 51

Badet, Regina, 6
Baker, Josephine, 43
Bakst, Leon, 9, 60, 61, 62, 63, 66, 67, 69, 70, 71, 75, 79, 80, 91, 111, 114, 117-118
Balanchine, George, xviii, 44, 46, 51, 116 (footnote)
Ballet Review, xviii
Ballet Russe de Monte Carlo, see Russian Ballet
Ballet Theater, 46, 48, 125
Banks, Richard, xix-xx
Barnes, Clive, xii (quoted)
Baylis, Lilian, 125
Beardsley, Aubrey, 61, 76, 83
Beaumont, Cyril, xii, 123
Beecham, Thomas, 64
Benavente, Jacinto, 143 (quoted)
Bendix, Max, 34
Benois, Alexandre, 61, 80, 118
Bernhardt, Sarah, 82
Bilbao, 139
Blanche, Jacques, 61
Bocher, Main, 54
Bolm, Adolph, 59, 72, 81
Boris, Ruthanna, 48

Bretón, Tomás, 150, 155
Buckle, Richard, 95 (footnote)
Butcher, Fanny, xii (quoted)

Carmencita, 137, 164
Carnaval (Schumann), 69-70, 75, 77, 78, 81, 82, 83, 84, 88, 117
Carnegie Hall, 18, 21, 26, 29-30
Cavalazzi, Malvina, 12-14, 24-25
Cecchetti, Enrico, 127
Celli, Vincenzo, 124, 127
Century Theatre, 80, 84
Cerito, Fanny, 172
Chabrier, Alexis Emmanuel, 137, 144, 145, 150, 151-152, 153, 155
Chase, Lucia, 125
Chujoy, Anatole, xvi (quoted)
Cléopâtre (Arensky), 27, 64, 75, 80, 81, 83
Collins, Janet, 43, 45
Collins, Lottie, 3
Copland, Aaron *(Billy The Kid),* 47
Craig, Gordon, 59, 78
Croce, Arlene, xviii (quoted)
Cunningham, Scott, xv (quoted)

Dafora, Asadata, 43
Damrosch, Walter, 15, 17, 18, 19-20, 21-22, 26
Dance Encyclopedia, xvi
Dance Index, xiv
Dance, June Walk, xviii
Danilova, Choura, 124
Davillier, Baron Charles *(l'Espagne),* 161-162
Debussy, Claude, 68, 69
   l'Après-midi d'un Faune, 27, 64, 67-69, 73, 75, 77, 79, 82, 88, 90, 94, 112, 117
   Jeux, 64, 73, 76, 108, 117, 174

179

Delibes, Léo, x, 171-178
   Coppélia, 95-98, 103, 128, 171, 174, 175, 177, 178 (footnote)
   Lakmé, 175-176
   La Source, 175
   Sylvia, 174, 175, 177
deMille, Agnes, xvii, 46, 47, 48, 49-56, 123, 124 (quoted), 129 (quoted)
   And Promenade Home, 52-56
   Allegro, 51
   Bloomer Girl, 51, 54
   Brigadoon, 51, 53
   Carousel, 51, 53
   Dance To The Piper, 49-52, 53
   Fall River Legend, 51
   Oklahoma!, 51, 53
   One Touch of Venus, 53
   Paint Your Wagon, 51
   Rodeo, 47, 51, 53
   Tally-Ho, 48, 51, 53
   Three Virgins And A Devil, 54
Denby, Edwin, xiii (quoted)
de Valois, Ninette, 51, 125
Diaghilev (Diaghileff), Serge de, 8, 9, 59, 60, 70, 79 (footnote), 80, 83, 85, 107, 111, 125, 127
Doboujinsky, 61
Dolin, Anton, 123-125, 126, 131 (footnote)
Doloretes, 138, 156
Doré, Gustave, 162
Dreiser, Theodore, 49-50
Duncan, Isadora, x, xiii-xiv, xvi, xix, 4, 5-6, 10, 15-29, 30, 32, 87, 103
Dunham, Katherine, 43

Edwards, Rhoda G., 158-159 (quoted)
Ellis, Havelock, 137, 138, 141, 142, 145, 147, 149, 150-151, 164, 167 (footnote)
Elman, Mischa, 125
Elssler, Fanny, 11, 103, 106, 149, 154, 166-167 (footnote), 172, 173

Fedorowsky, Theodore, 61, 118
Finck, H.T. *(Spain and Morocco)*, 153-154, 159
Fokina, Vera, 59, 72
Fokine, Michel, 8, 27, 47, 59, 71, 72, 73-74, 75, 76, 80, 83, 88, 111
Ford, Anne, 164
Ford, Richard *(Gatherings From Spain)*, 137, 141, 142 (footnote), 143, 146, 147, 155-156
Franklin, Frederick, 48
Fremstad, Olive, 5, 76, 86
Fuertes, Soriano, 148, 150

Fuller, Loie, xiii, 4-5, 15, 30, 32-34

Gallup, Donald, xi
Ganne, Louis, 26
Garden, Mary, xiv, xvi, 6, 43, 125
Gautier, Théophile, xii, 69, 99, 104, 152-153, 154-155, 172
Geltzer, Katerina (Catherine), 8, 81, 104-107
Genée, Adeline, 5, 103-104
Gershwin, George, 51
Glanville-Hicks, Peggy, 45
Glazunow (Glazounov), Alexander, 102
   Bacchanale, 103
   Raymonda, 100
   The Seasons, 101
Gluck, Christoph W., 16, 18, 21-22, 72, 119
   Iphigénie en Aulide, 16, 24
   Iphigénie en Tauride, 16
   Orfeo, 21, 24, 30, 127
Goetzl, Anselm, 90
Golovine, A., 61, 111, 114
Gontcharowa, Nathalie, 61
Gosse, Edmund, 68
Goudeket, Maurice, 55
Graham, Martha, xvii-xviii, 43, 50-51, 54
Grisi, Carlotta, 99-101, 103, 172

Hacket, Alice Payne, xvi
Hahn, Reynaldo, 71-72
   Le Dieu Bleu, 64, 70-72, 75, 108
Hale, Philip, 149, 150, 161
Harburg, E.Y., 54
Harris, William Hubbard, 65-66 (quoted)
Haskell, Arnold, xii
Heine, Heinrich, 99-100, 138
Henderson, W.J., 66 (quoted)
Hertz, Alfred, 110
Hill, Edward Burlingham, 113 (quoted)
Hill, J. Leubrie, 36-38
Hinkson, Mary, 43
Holder, Geoffrey, 43
Horne, Lena, 45
Horton, Lester, 44-45
Huneker, James, 164 (quoted)
Hurok, Sol, 125

Imperio, Pastora, 143
Isherwood, Christopher, 49

Jablonski, Edward, xvii (quoted)
Jacob's Pillow, 45
Jones, Robert E., 91

Karsavina, Tamara, 8, 59, 66, 67, 70, 77, 78-79, 81, 83, 85, 103, 110
Kaye, Nora, 46, 48
Kchessinska, Mathilde, 124-125
Kellner, Bruce, ix, xiii (quoted)
Kidd, Michael, 56
Kirstein, Lincoln, xvii (quoted)
Klatte, Wilhelm, 91
Knopf, Alfred A., xv
Kochno, Boris, 79 (footnote)
Krehbiel, H.E. *(Afro-American Folksongs)*, 112, 144-145, 148
Kriza, John, 46
Kurtz, Efrem, 129 (quoted)

Lac des Cygnes, Le, see Tchaikowsky
Lafontaine, Henry Cart de, 157-158 (quoted)
Laing, Hugh, 46
Lang, Harold, 46
Lang, Pearl, 52
Lavallade, Carmen de, 44-45
Lerman, Leo, xviii-xix (quoted)
Lifar, Serge, 8
Lindy Hop, xiv, 38-40
Little Egypt, 3-4
Llobet, Miguel, 146-147
Long, Avon, 43
Lopoukova, Lydia, 82
Loring, Eugene, 46, 47, 51
Lueders, Edward, xiv (quoted)

Magriel, Paul, xii (quoted)
Mahler, Gustav, 11
Mallarmé, Stéphane, 67, 77
Manhattan Casino, 39
Manhattan Opera House, xvi, 90, 91, 95 (footnote), 125
Mapleson, Charles, 13, 24
Marinoff, Fania, xv
Markova, Alicia, xviii, 9, 47, 123-131, 167 (footnote)
Marseillaise, 24, 25, 28, 40
Martin, John, xii, xiv (quoted), 129 (quoted)
Massine, Leonide, 8, 59, 79, 80-81, 90, 94-95 (footnote)
Mauri, Rosita, 172
Maxwell, Elsa, 129 (quoted)
Metropolitan Opera House, 4, 7, 11, 12-14, 15, 17, 22, 26, 30, 32, 43, 45, 84, 86, 95, 96, 97, 99, 102, 104, 106, 176
Midas (Steinberg), 64, 74, 75, 78, 110
Mitchell, Arthur, 43
Mitchell, James, 53
Moeller, Philip, xiv, xv (quoted)

Molière, Jean-Baptiste, 156 (quoted), 167 (footnote)
Molina, Amalia, 143, 144
Montague-Nathan, M., 113-114 (quoted)
Monteaux, Pierre, 90
Mordkin, Mikail (Michael), xiii, 8, 11, 95-102, 103, 106, 108
My Friend from Kentucky, 36-37

Narcisse (Tcherepnine), 27, 64, 75, 82, 88, 89, 91, 108, 117, 174
Nassau Dancing, 40-42
New Theatre, The, 98
New York City Ballet, xviii, xix-xx, 43, 116 (footnote)
Nijinsky, Waslav, xiii, xiv, xviii, xix, 8, 9, 45, 48, 59, 60, 67, 69, 70-71, 73, 75, 76, 77-79, 79-95, 98 (footnote), 110, 112, 117, 118, 137

Oswald, Genevieve, 9 (footnote)

Page, Ruth, 48
Park Theatre, 137, 141-142 (footnote)
Papillons (Schumann), 60, 69, 75, 81, 118
Pas de Quatre (Pugni), 48, 127
Paul, Mimi, xviii
Pavillion d'Armide, Le (Tcherepnine), 72, 83, 108, 118
Pavlowa (Pavlova), Anna, xiii, xvi, xviii, 7, 8, 11, 15, 47, 78, 81, 83, 87, 95-104, 116-117, 128, 149, 178 (footnote)
Petipa, Marius, 47
Pillar of Fire (Schönberg), 48
Piltz, Maria, 112
Primus, Pearl, 43
Prince Igor (Borodine), 61, 72-73, 75, 80, 81, 84, 108
Princesse Enchantée, La, see Tchaikowsky
Prude, Walter, 54-55

Rambert, Marie, 51
Ravel, Maurice, 111, 155
    Daphnis et Chloë, 8, 27, 62, 63, 64, 75, 81, 108, 174
Reed, Janet, 46, 48
Reinach, Salomon, 71
Revalles, Flore, 82-83
Rimsky-Korsakow (Korsakov), Nicholas A., 11, 64, 67, 69, 80, 102, 108, 111, 115, 116 (footnote)
    Golden Cock, 60, 61, 67, 78, 108
    Sadko, 75, 81, 90

181

Scheherazade, 11, 27, 61, 62, 63, 64, 66, 67, 75, 77, 80, 81, 84, 88-89, 90, 91, 101, 117
Rite of Spring, see Stravinsky
Rittman, Trude, 54
Robbins, Jerome, 46, 47, 48, 51, 54, 56
 Fancy Free, 47, 51
 Interplay, 47, 48
Robert, Grace *(Borzoi Book of Ballets),* 46-49
Robinson, Bill, 42-43
Rodin, Auguste, 69
Roerich, Nicholas, 61, 72, 75, 80, 118
Romantic Age (Bellini), 127-128
Romeo and Juliet (Delius), 126, 127
Rouge et Noir (Shostakovitch), 123, 126, 127
Rubinstein, Artur, 125
Rubinstein, Ida, 81, 83, 117
Russian Ballet (Ballet Russe de Monte Carlo), xiii, 8, 9, 27, 46, 48, 59-79, 80-107, 111, 117-119, 125, 135-136, 139
Russian Folk-Tales (Rolston), 115

Sacre du Printemps, Le, see Stravinsky
Sadler's Wells Ballet, 9
Saint-Saëns, Camille, 174, 176 (quoted)
Salome (Schmitt), 61, 78
Sangalli, Rita, 172, 177
Sert, José-Maria, 63
Shaw, George B., 60
Sherwin, Louis, 141
Skirt Dance, 3-4
Sokolova, Lydia, 124
Souday, Paul, 69
Soudeikine, Serge, 61, 118
Spectre de la Rose, Le (Weber), 69, 75, 82, 86-87, 88, 117
Spessiva, Olga, 125
St. Denis, Ruth, 7, 177
Stein, Gertrude, x-xi, 116 (footnote), 148-149, 166
 Autobiography of Alice B. Toklas, 116 (footnote)
 Bee Time Vine, 166 (footnote)
 The Making of Americans, xi (quoted)
Stettheimer, Florine, xv-xvi, xx
Stier, Theodore, 102
Stravinsky (Strawinsky), Igor, x, 8, 64, 75, 80, 84, 107-116
 Firebird, The, 64, 80, 81, 82, 84, 111, 114-116, 126
 Nightingale, The, 110-111

Petrouchka, 64, 75, 76, 78, 80, 81, 82, 84, 86, 88, 89, 91, 109-110, 111, 113-114, 116 (footnote), 118, 174
 Sacrifice to the Spring (Sacre du Printemps, Le, Rite of Spring), 8, 40, 61, 64, 73, 75, 94, 109, 111-113, 116 (footnote), 118
Strauss, Richard, 64, 74, 80, 91, 110, 119
 Legend of Joseph, 8, 60, 62, 63, 64, 74, 75, 78, 80, 108, 110, 118, 174
 Salome, xvi, 31-32, 78
 Till Eulenspiegel, 88, 90-91
Suarès, André, 171-172 (quoted)
Sylphides, Les (Chopin), 5, 11-12, 47, 69, 75, 76, 78, 82, 88, 89, 123, 126
Symons, Arthur, 92 (quoted), 156-157, 159-160

Taglioni, Marie, 11, 47, 103, 106, 128, 172, 173
Talin, Nikita, 48
Tchaikowsky (Tschaikowsky), Peter, 47, 64, 104-106, 108
 Aleko, 127
 Marche Slave, 25-26
 Sleeping Beauty (La Princesse Enchantée), 9, 82, 88, 89, 106, 126
 Swan Lake (Le Lac de Cygnes), xvi, 8, 104-107, 125
Tchernicheva, Lubov, 82, 90
Tempest, Marie, 86, 103
Terry, Walter, 178 (footnote)
Thamar (Balakirew), 64, 65-66, 75, 80, 81, 83, 117
Thicknesse, Philip, xii, 162-164
Toscanini, Arturo, 110
Tudor, Antony, 46, 51
Turney, Matt, 43

Valverde, Joaquin, 137, 139
Vision of Salome, 29, 30-32
Vuillermoz, Emile, 173 (quoted), 176
Vuillier, Gaston *(A History of Dancing),* 161-162

Walker, Aida Overton, 5, 36, 42
Walker, George, 5, 34-36, 42
Walkowitz, Abraham, 28-29
West, Mae, 5, 95 (footnote)
Williams, Bert, 5, 34-36, 42
Wilson, John C., 54
Wycherly, Margaret, 91

Zambelli, Carlotta, 6
Ziegfeld, Florenz, 38, 136

182